A STOLE
IS A TOWEL

A STOLE
IS A TOWEL

*Lessons Learned in the
Parish Ministry
by*

MARTHA B. KRIEBEL

THE PILGRIM PRESS
New York

Copyright © 1988 The Pilgrim Press
All rights reserved

Library of Congress Cataloging-in-Publication Data

Kriebel, Martha B., 1935–
    A stole is a towel: lessons learned in the parish ministry /
by Martha B. Kriebel.

    ISBN 0-8298-0792-6
    1. Clergy—Office.   2. Pastoral theology.   3. Women clergy.
4. Kriebel, Martha B., 1935– . I. Title.
BV660.2.K75   1988
253'.088042—dc19   88-22429
                                                        CIP

The Pilgrim Press, 132 West 31 Street, New York, NY 10001

CONTENTS

PREFACE

A front page headline in the December 24, 1986 issue of the *Wall Street Journal* announced:

UNEQUAL RIGHTS

Women Ministers Face
A Host of Obstacles
In Chosen Profession

They Often Can't Find Jobs
Leading Congregations,
Suffer Pay Discrimination

The Bible's Sexist Language

The article's interviews chronicled the now familiar data.

In response to statistics and headlines, books have been and are being written that describe pain, voice protest, advocate change. Books about Christian feminism, goddess theology, the ordination of women, inclusive language— and now, another book? No! This one is *different*. It is more than one person's response to what is being experienced by women whose stories were featured in the *Wall Street Journal*. This book is like a laboratory notebook kept by a person who is both the researcher and the research, and the data is an accumulation of more than a quarter century of learning. (Doesn't that sound impressive!) But more important, this book suggests ways to work through problems that keep women from being ordained to the ministry and called or named to a parish.

Just another book? I urge you to discover this book's difference and purpose.

ACKNOWLEDGMENTS

Resources I have quoted and people to whom I am indebted are listed in the chapters, but the references lack the most important detail: appreciation. "Thank you!"

There is one person whose name has not been given, the person who turned my scribbled notes into a typed manuscript: Mary E. Remig—wife, mother, grandmother; church secretary who is really an unpaid associate pastor without title; neighbor, friend, counselor; servant of Christ—whose service enables me to know the joys of the parish ministry.

INTRODUCTION

When Bela Vassady was professor of theology at Lancaster Theological Seminary (Pennsylvania), he often responded to a first-year student's question with the remark, "We'll get to that next year."

In the second year a question raised in class sometimes elicited the same answer, "We'll get to that next year." And so that next year, the last year, turned into a challenge to devise the strategy for the final inquiry that would prompt the answer Dr. Vassady would, at last, give, for there would be no "next year." An anxious class of seniors turned silent as the person primed to raise a question spoke up and then joined the silence so as not to miss a word. And this is what they heard: "You'll learn that in the field." (The "field" meant the congregation and community to which the seniors, soon to be graduates, would be going.)

Dr. Vassady's answer was received and submerged under a false nod of appreciation that covered a mix of resentment and frustration—until the inquirers began to work "in the field." Then words received as an inappropriate joke proved to be an astute, caring professor's wise counsel. The "field" would prove to be both an instructor and a course of study for lifelong learning.

Now, after almost thirty years in that "field," I can say, "Dr. Vassady, you were right!" Many lessons are learned while serving as a pastor of a congregation, far more learning than a seminary's curriculum could accommodate, or even anticipate. And when the pastor is a woman, the parish is a teacher of lessons that are taught only in the "field." The chapters that follow are my "classroom notes" on lessons learned in the parish ministry.

A STOLE
IS A TOWEL

1 • VISIBILITY

The Classroom

Being called to serve as pastor of a congregation in 1979 proved to be unlike the first call to the first parish in 1959. In 1959 a congregation of more than 600 members was presented with two candidates who, if elected, would be the first clergy couple to appear in the parish and in the denomination. No wonder the Sunday morning attendance was so high when the couple began to take turns supplying two months before the scheduled election! (This procedure would be frowned on today, but at that time it was an innocent arrangement and a "classroom" for a lesson that arrangement would teach.)

When the congregation met to vote on the clergy couple candidates, of the more than 100 who cast a ballot, only four voted no.

Two years later, when my husband submitted his resignation to expand his part-time teaching in the local high school to full time, and a new election was scheduled, to vote on calling the remaining pastor as sole pastor, the vote was unanimous.

But twenty years later a congregation voting on a candidate registered a different margin. Because I was the candidate under consideration, the size of the negative vote (almost 10 percent of the count) concerned me. I had come to them with above-average credentials: thirteen years in the parish ministry and seven years on a regional denominational staff (Pennsylvania Southeast Conference, United Church of Christ). Each period of service had references that would impress a pastoral search committee. The parish years were filled with community involvement and expanded church programs that attracted new members and their contributions of talents and dollars; the most impressive "celebration" was the quarter-million-dollar building program, beginning with no funds but only a mortgage, which was burned in six years. And then there were the additions to the résumé during the Conference staff years: evangelism research and resources, exposure to health and welfare and social concerns, ecumenical ventures, the less honored but essential experiences of pouring oil on troubled church waters and smoothing ruffled ecclesiastical feathers, the distinction of being the first ordained woman elected to a Conference staff in our denomination. Why, then, such a high negative vote? Why were there so many nos?

When I thought about the circumstances at the time of each of the elections, 1959 and 1979, I saw the two contrasting experiences as a "classroom" where a pastor, especially a pastor who is a woman, learns the first lesson taught in the setting of a parish.

The Lesson

In 1959 a congregation had had time to see a candidate serving in the office of pastor, at least the dimensions of that office that are visible during a Sunday morning service of worship, and after the service there was time to visit, to talk, to listen, and to look at each other.

In 1979 there was no opportunity for the congregation to see the candidate in a parish setting. As a member of the Conference staff, I was visible only to local church members who were elected delegates to the Conference's Annual Meeting, or to a congregation when invited to be a guest preacher, or to people as a retreat or workshop leader who did her "thing," but nothing associated with a woman serving as a pastor, and a congregation reacting, resonating, responding to my ministry.

Without that visibility I had no credibility as a candidate for the parish ministry. Nor did I nurture support for other women being denied ordination to the ministry by those who contend that "women should be silent in the church." A woman who accepted that silence as her role in a congregation said she was glad I was serving on the Conference staff; in that position I was no longer going against the Bible! I wasn't doing what only men should do—serve as pastor. I was just going around talking to Christians; the Conference position saved a congregation from being contaminated by the ministry of a woman! Her reasoning reinforced the lesson taught by the 1979 election experience. That lesson, in one word, is VISIBILITY—the need for a clergy woman to be visible long before seeking a call to a parish and all during the candidating process.

The book *Women of the Cloth*, by Jackson W. Carroll, Barbara Hargrove, and Adair T. Lummis, and the United Presbyterian Church, USA, booklet *Women in Ministry* are filled with references to visibility and its implementation at three levels: during seminary, when names of candidates are submitted to a congregation searching for a pastor, during the call process.

A SEMINARIAN'S VISIBILITY
IN A CONGREGATION

Visibility during seminary days is a need confirmed by personal experiences as a seminarian and now as a pastor whose congregation believes that it is part of *their* ministry to "educate a seminarian."

Three years ago our congregation welcomed a woman seminarian who was in her senior year. As spring approached, the inquiry began to be raised, "Have you heard from a church yet?" The attitude during that time was: "If they aren't enthused, we'll personally convince them!" That enthusiasm carried me back to the late 1950s, when I was anxiously waiting for a church to work through the call process. In the senior year of seminary my Sundays were filled supplying a congregation as its "Senior Seminarian," a title given to the person who conducted the worship service on alternate Sundays when the pastor was at another location in a two-church charge. Because the congregation seldom had visitors to welcome, faces of those who were not the "regulars" were easily spotted. On my alternate Sundays with them I saw two, three, four new faces—a pulpit committee listening, looking, reacting to a woman conducting a service of worship and—the most critical observation—preaching a sermon. Within three months a call followed.

A local congregation welcoming and responding to a seminarian provides a necessary service, visibility, and with that visibility the setting that may encourage another congregation to ask that student for the ministry to be its future pastor.

OTHER OCCASIONS FOR VISIBILITY

During seminary years there are other times and settings that become opportunities for visibility. One seminary professor moved the classroom to a denomination's annual theological colloquy. Students not only took notes on three days of presentations and discussions and helped to write a position paper, but also they mingled with clergy and laity. They were visible—as seminarians. After one of the discussions a layperson commented on the maturity of the students, especially the women. "Have you noticed how perceptive they are and how much they know about the Bible, theology, world issues, and the very practical matters of a parish?" Then she exclaimed, "How fortunate our congregation would be to have one of these students as our future pastor!" An exclamation prompted by observation.

In Associations and Conferences of the United Church of Christ (UCC) seminarians are invited to the meetings, their presence is often acknowledged through a standing introduction, and their participation on committees is encouraged as their time permits. How many other opportunities are there for visibility? Conference, seminar, symposium, and colloquy are occasions for seminarians to be involved and, through that involvement, to be seen. These occasions take on special significance for a woman.

THE ROLE OF THE JUDICATORY

"When names are submitted to a congregation searching for a pastor" moves the responsibility from a seminary, seminarian, and local congregation to judicatory personnel. The United Presbyterian Church, USA, provides the research to prove how essential this effort is. Since the mid-1970s women's names have been submitted along with male clergy's, and some churches have called women. *Women of the Cloth* also indicated that intentional efforts by judicatory staff to urge the consideration of a woman as pastor do not meet with reaction and rejection. The opposite is true, turning "Consider a woman, well, I don't know" to "Maybe" to "OK. Let's try it!"

The bishop of an Anglican diocese in South Saskatchewan, Canada, said, "When I send a woman to a church to be their rector, they request a woman the next time they have a vacancy." That judicatory executive is to be commended for his action, but when the placing of a pastor is by "being elected" rather than by "being sent," the names that are submitted to a committee of the congregation for their consideration need to be carefully chosen, especially the names of women.

During my days as a member of a UCC Conference staff, pastoral search committees were overheard saying, "They (the Conference) stick a woman's name on the list. It's a denominational rule, that says we've got to consider women as well as men. But we don't look at her name! We forget about the women."

To change from "forgetting" to "looking" and "considering" means the names submitted must be more than paperwork. Jackson W. Carroll and Robert L. Wilson, in *Too Many Pastors? The Clergy Job Market*, detail the time-consuming responsibility placed on a judicatory executive. She or he must personally, or through delegated staff, know and be able to recommend candidates; visit seminaries; be acquainted with the strengths, weaknesses, and special interests of students for the ministry; and know the needs and situations of churches seeking pastors. Then, when a woman's name appears on the list submitted to a search committee, because she can be given serious consideration, she is a potential candidate, not just a name to "forget."

Judicatorial intervention, usually dubbed "affirmative action," is an essential service to provide visibility, and this time-consuming effort on the part of denominational executives has a complementary action. A well-trained pastoral search committee.

TRAINING THE
PASTORAL SEARCH COMMITTEE

During the call process a committee needs an agenda, a procedure, and resources. The United Presbyterian Church provides a model to emulate to bring a woman's name before the committee members. Through its Women in Ministry Project and such audiovisuals as "A New Wave Breaking: Women Are Ministers" and "The Opening Door," search committees are guided in considering women as well as men to fill a pastoral vacancy. Through questionnaires, role playing, and case studies, sharing of attitudes, impressions, assumptions—real and imagined— the members share their thoughts and then deal with them. The congregation is also helped to vote without prejudice when a candidate is proposed. This facet of the word visibility may lead to far more than calling a woman to fill a pastoral vacancy. It is an exercise in uncovering and examining unconscious, subtle impressions about gender and sexuality that we may impose on others and use to define our own self-worth.

My election as pastor in 1979 became more than a private "classroom" for a lesson taught through one word—

visibility. A pastoral search committee was also educated, and they carried their lesson to the entire congregation—which meant that they had to design their own teaching tools and lesson plans. The resources now available for search committees did not exist at that time, nor did they know that the large negative vote cast against a woman would be explained by the Presbyterians a few years later. By the 1980s there would be data showing that the more educated the membership is, the larger the negative vote (for a woman candidate) will be. It is a rural congregation, with a high-school-level education or less, who tend to welcome a woman as their pastor. The congregation voting in 1979 was an unrecorded statistic that confirmed that finding, a church with a historic tie to a church-related college, its across-the-street neighbor, and employer of many of its members. The committee, not knowing that the negative rumblings heard around the parish, campus, bridge parties, and dinner tables were normal, proceeded to work out their own plan. And what a commendable plan it was!

Six individuals *personally* spoke with *every* member of the congregation who was well enough or close enough to be contacted. By the Sunday morning of the election the committee was able to predict how many negative votes would be cast, for they knew from their conversations what each member's hesitation or reaction was. But much more than that was learned. An airing of attitudes and opinions about a pastoral candidate's gender opened each member to a personal examination, a test, on the subject of what it means to be male, female, clergy, laity.

To give visibility to a woman who is a seminarian or ordained clergy seeking a call to a congregation or an agency of the church is a learning experience for that person *and* for everyone who votes. That is what I learned when an election became the "classroom" and the tally of votes became the "teacher"—for me and for all who voted yes or no.

2 • IDENTITY

The Classroom

One Wednesday night, at a community's lenten service, the sermon was preached by a young woman who was pastor of the local Methodist church. She is about two inches taller than I am, has brunette hair, with long curls that touch her shoulders. My hair style is short, and nature is frosting my once reddish blonde waves. She does not wear glasses; I do. She sings soprano and speaks in a high-pitched voice. I sing alto and speak at a much lower pitch and in a style that bears no resemblance to hers. She wears a clerical robe and stole that are entirely different from mine. She is single; I am married. She is a recent seminary graduate; my graduation and ordination preceded hers by twenty-five years.

After that Wednesday night lenten service a man I have known for years, who is a friend of our family and often spends time in our home, and has worshiped at Trinity Church, where I am now pastor, came to me and said, "Martha, I thought that was you standing in the pulpit tonight!"

The only likeness we share is that we are both women!

His friendly remark became another classroom teaching another lesson.

The Lesson

A woman is a woman, and a woman clergyperson is a non-person. When you've seen one, you've seen them all—which means that women in the ministry pay a high price for being viewed with ambiguity and anonymity. The price may be paid in a number of ways.

One woman's appearance, personal conduct, or style of ministry may be used as a reference to and judgment of every woman. A parishioner who said he wasn't impressed by *one* woman minister he had met let that one woman form his opinion that any woman would be a poor pastor. His impression reinforces my plea for the visibility of women, beginning in seminary, so that they may be seen in the setting of a parish, practicing the work of a pastor, doing what male seminarians do in a local congregation, and then perhaps women will be recognized and evaluated as individuals.

Many other subtleties are involved in the price a woman pays because she is a woman. The dominant pronoun he, its use as *the* pronoun for God, and all the biblical and theological ramifications that stand on that choice dictate to some that the word rabbi or clergy comes in one gender, and it isn't feminine! By that definition of ministry a woman pays the price of being a non-person; there is no such thing as a woman clergyperson. Her identity is to have no identity.

ADDRESS

Twenty-five years ago this message was conveyed through forms of address. Even in those denominations that ordained women for the ministry, a woman was addressed as "Miss" or "Mrs.," while the clergyman was "Reverend!" I see this subtlety returning as Christians whose fundamentalist theology refuses to accept women as ordained clergy show their conviction when addressing a letter or introducing a woman who is ordained to the ministry. My first reaction was to do a slow burn by keeping a lid of politeness on top of my resentment. "What are titles anyway?" I would argue with myself. "Didn't Jesus have stern words for clergy in his day who insisted on being called by ministerial forms of address? Didn't he refuse to be identified by the 'Reverend' of that culture ('Rabbi' or 'Teacher')?" "Martha," I'd say to myself, "Shame on you! Your pride and arrogance are showing!" Then I'd say, "I'm sorry, God; forgive me!" a few times under my breath, while my resentment continued to boil! Finally I lifted that lid of politeness and looked inside, ready to identify the feelings that fired my personal caldron. Was the heat generated by pride or arrogance? Or was it another price paid by a clergy woman?

Now when I ask myself, "Am *I* the problem?" I answer, "No, the problem belongs to everyone." It is one more subtlety a woman minister encounters as the price paid for being a woman in the ministry. And because it is, I now work to keep the fire of my personal resentment from burning. When I detect a discriminating introduction, I politely correct the introducer. For example, I say, "Please feel free to call me by the same title you call your pastor (a clergyman)." Recently a mailing came to our home. For years the addresser had sent correspondence to my husband and me: "Revs. Howard and Martha Kriebel," which is the way we suggest our mail be addressed. The sender is a conservative Christian resort that has just undergone a shift to a biblical stance that rejects the ordination of women. The shift was translated into the words on the envelope, no longer "Revs. Howard and Martha Kriebel," but "Rev. and Mrs. Howard Kriebel." My first reaction was to forget about it, but the fires of resentment didn't let that response work! My second reaction was to turn my irritation into the energy to write a letter and request an address correction because, as I explained, "both of us are ordained ministers."

It's such a small matter, the matter of how clergy are addressed, but it is not irrelevant. It is an exercise in learning to identify a clergywoman as a person, just as much of a person as a clergyman. At times it is an entertaining exercise, resisted with, "We can't call you 'Reverend'; you're a woman!" Or the wrestlings of Episcopalians who ordain women and then wonder how to address them. If rectors, who in the past have all been male, are called "Father," is a female priest called "Mother"? On one occasion I heard myself introduced as, "If she were Roman Catholic, she'd be a priestess." Some would dismiss the search to find suitable titles and forms of address as a ridiculous pursuit, but I no longer permit this exercise to be dismissed. It is part of wrestling with the identity of being a woman ordained to the ministry.

DRESS

When a woman conducted her first worship service as a minister, she wore clerical garb over her dress. The congregation was accustomed to seeing clergymen wearing this garb. A man was asked what his impression was; his answer: "Ankles! For the first time I saw ankles in the chancel!" When a clergywoman dressed in a clerical shirt and suit walked into a meeting of ordained ministers, one man wearing a similar clerical shirt forcefully pushed her out of the room, shouting, "You have no right to be here!" Clergy dress is a discussion that invites a mixed response. Some would dismiss the entire subject as too trivial to make an issue, but I see it as another subtlety that new vestments may be turning into an ecclesiastical fashion show.

In our UCC Conference the 1987 annual meeting included a procession of all styles of cassocks, pulpit robes, albs, stoles, etc. worn by the clergy. I proudly modeled my vestment, which is a silent protest few knew to identify. To recognize the style requires a knowledge of sixteenth-century Reformed Church history. The clergy parade was a colorful, laughable display, more like a circus than a fashion show, proving that it is "open season" in the world of clergy apparel.

With all the "costumes" to choose from, what does a woman wear? I take that question seriously, and wear the sign of the office to which I have been ordained, not to keep clergy apparel companies in business, but to identify my ministry, believing that clothes *do* make the clergywoman as well as the man. And if a denomination has its garb that is a sign of ordination, then an ordained woman should wear that sign, even at the risk of having her ankles show in the chancel or of being accosted, as one woman was.

I wear the collar, the robe, the stole when in the chancel, the clerical blouse or shirt with a suit or skirt or dress when going about the work of a pastor. I wear the sign of the office to which I have been ordained. (I return to this subject in chapter 3.)

14

SCRIPTURE

But the real lesson I have learned in the parish classroom where the subject is a clergywoman's identity, is testing; the emotional examination of the references a person uses to identify a woman who is a minister or a student for the ministry. What impressions are behind the judgment that withholds ordination from women? Biblical quotations are a certain reference. What verses is a person using to identify a woman as an unacceptable candidate for the ministry? A young woman seminarian dismissed those references as "ridiculous" at a clergy conference held in 1986. She argued that no one pays attention to the apostle Paul's words about women being silent in the church (1 Timothy 2:11–15). Other clergywomen did not know whether to call her opinion naiveté, or to take it as a sign that she needed more courses on the Bible, especially Paul's New Testament letters. To ignore the Bible as a source that identifies women as unfit for the ministry is either naiveté or ignorance, for the Bible is *the* source for proof texts quoted to prove that women are committed to silence in the church.

Because the scriptures have traditionally been termed a Christian's "rule for faith and practice" (a statement often addressed to a layperson as well as to a minister when ordained and installed to an office in the church), an individual must be "tested" as to his or her interpretation of biblical references regarding women. That is another teaching chore associated with identity—exposing and examining the verses a person uses to determine a woman's place in the ordained ministry. And this chore is directed not only toward "them," those who argue a woman must be denied ordination, but also toward clergywomen—and their self-image, their identity, especially when a woman reads, or has read to her: "Women should learn in silence and all humility. I do not allow women to teach or to have authority over men; they must keep quiet. For Adam was created first [1 Tim. 2:11–13, TEV]." This "ammunition" is quoted from Paul's letter, if a person wants to put a woman in "her place." (The later verse 15 reinforces the "woman's place is in the home" adage until the alternate translation is read, as footnoted in *The New English Bible*, "brought safely through childbirth"—a promise of God's protection rather than punishment.) 1 Corinthians 14:34–35 is another reference sometimes used.

I was publicly introduced to 1 Timothy 2:11–15 at a community's Thanksgiving service a few years ago. The host pastor, serving as liturgist, read the ecumenical lectionary for the occasion—Isaiah 61:10–11; 1 Timothy 2:1–8; Luke 12:22–31—with one exception. He did not stop after the eighth verse in the second lesson, but read the entire chapter.

I also want the women to be modest and sensible about their clothes and to dress properly; not with fancy hair styles or with gold ornaments or pearls or expensive dresses, but with good deeds, as is proper for women who claim to be religious. Women should learn in silence and all humility. I do not allow them to teach or to have authority over men; they must keep quiet. For Adam was created first, and then Eve. And it was not Adam who was deceived; it was the woman who was deceived and broke God's law. But a woman will be saved through having children, if she perseveres in faith and love and holiness, with modesty.

—1 Timothy 2:9–15, TEV

The congregation of Episcopalians, Evangelical Congregationalists, Lutherans, Methodists, Roman Catholics, and United Church of Christ shifted back and forth in the pews and silently spoke a body language of confusion, anger, disbelief. Was the extended reading intended? The preacher was a clergywoman (myself)!

Fortunately there were some rubrics and congregational responses that preceded the sermon. That gave me time to attempt a response that would defuse the atmosphere. When I stepped into the pulpit and looked at rows of confused, embarrassed, flushed faces, I began, "Our brother read verses that extended the reading from Paul's First Letter to Timothy from verse eight to the end of the second chapter. After hearing that lesson commanding women to be silent, I suppose the only appropriate thing for me to do is to sit down and let you go on with the rest of the service! But that is *not* what that letter instructs me to do."

I attempted a few minutes' summary of volumes of interpretive studies, suggesting that as Paul urged Philemon to accept a runaway slave into his household, replacing the sentence of death for a disobedient servant with forgiveness prompted by Christ's law of love, so must we continue to apply that law, moving from slavery to the humanness and worth of women as well as men.

Then I turned to the unscheduled verses and said, "At the time that letter was written, Hebrew children learned the laws, prayers, and festivals of their faith in the home. At the age of six, boys continued their education in the synagogue school; at twelve the best students, like the apostle Paul, went on to study for the rabbinate. Paul was saying to women who had *no formal education*, 'be silent'; his words applied to our time would be to tell people with a kindergarten education that they cannot teach college-level courses."

"Because," I added, "education in our society is for women and men, and I have been privileged to pursue the learning that equips me to preach, I have no excuse. I must proceed with the sermon for this service." To chuckles of relief, I thanked the host clergyman, who had provided the opportunity for me to preach on a text I had never had an occasion to use. Then I went on with the sermon intended for the Thanksgiving service, silently giving thanks for having pursued a personal study of verses like 1 Timothy 2:11–15 ever since I was ordained to the Christian ministry.

"Ever since I was ordained" may seem a little late to begin such a study, and now I look back and realize that another facet to the subject of identity preceded the question of a woman's right to be a clergyperson. Even though all the role models had been men, their gender had not raised a barrier to my pursuing a similar ministry in the church. That is a not-so-unique perception confirmed by *Women of the Cloth* and interviews with clergywomen who reported that their mentors were men who were either their pastor or father, relative, or close friend, data that suggests the work of pastor may not be perceived as being "for men only" by the people who constitute a clergyman's congregation or family.

For me, however, there was a prior identification. I found my way into a church vocation by a circuitous route, through medicine to ministry. Since the age of twelve I had planned to be a doctor, and a visible encouragement was nearby, Women's Medical College (now the Pennsylvania College of Medicine) in the East Falls section of Philadelphia. In the summer I'd bike to the hospital's emergency room and watch women with their black medical bags and stethoscopes hurrying in and out of cars and doors. I'd say, "In the not-too-distant future I'll be one of them. Doing what they are doing." Then a second interest dawned: religion. It began with a church that urged its youth "to make a decision for Christ." I went to the church's summer camp, attended the closing camp fire, filled in the Commitment Card with its three questions, but never checked the first: "I accept Jesus Christ as my personal Savior" (with space to fill in the day and hour). The second question about striving to live a Christlike life was OK. And the third was a commitment I could and did make without hesitation: "I commit myself to full-time Christian service."

Years later, when reading the historical section of the 1902 edition of the *Heidelberg Catechism*, I realized why I had difficulty accepting the directive stated in the first question. These words in the catechism held the answer to my hesitation:

No need to doubt your conversion, your change of heart, because you cannot tell the day when it took place, as many profess to do. It did not take place in a day, or you might tell it. It is the growth of years (Mark 4:26–28), and therefore all the more reliable. You cannot tell when you learned to walk, talk, think and work. You do not know when you learned to love your earthly father, much less the heavenly.

This is the Reformed doctrine of "getting religion." We get religion, not in bulk but little by little. Just as we get natural life and strength, so spiritual life and strength, day by day.

Now, with the interviews reported in *Women of the Cloth* on one hand and those lines well marked on page 184 in the *Heidelberg Catechism* on the other, I understand why I could not answer the first question, and why I cherished that edition. I could have read and marked a more recent printing, but this one was my father's. He was one of my mentors. He was both an ordained deacon and the Financial Secretary, and the congregation's joke was that the church door couldn't be locked until our family left!

I found no difficulty in merging the thought of being a doctor with the commitment to full-time Christian service;

I would be a medical missionary serving in India, perhaps Vellore, where women doctors were needed in a Hindu society that prohibited men from attending women. It all seemed to work out so well even before I began to work through the courses. And then there was that junior year at college! It started with courses I had not been able to fit in because of all the premedical requirements; now most were taken or could be scheduled, and there was time for other interests. Of course, the choices would be Bible, church history, and world religions. There was also a course on Christian classics, a study of *The Fellowship of the Saints,* compiled by Thomas S. Kepler. The course became my identity crisis. By the end of my junior year I was on my way to months of "dark nights of the soul"! That "darkness" settled in as I began to analyze my vocational choice, which seemed to be so intact—until I asked myself, "Must you go to India to be a good Christian? Aren't Christian doctors needed here? What is the difference between being a medical missionary and a medical doctor who is a committed Christian?" And then *the* question worked its way to the top of the list, "What do I really mean when I say I want to be 'in full-time Christian service'? Is it medicine, or is it the ministry?" There! The real issue was out in the open. The real identity crisis was identified. But I did not act until the last month in my senior year. I had been accepted by two medical schools and made it appear that my dilemma was to decide which one to attend. That was a cover; the unchanged issue was medical school or seminary? At first I reasoned, "I will go to seminary, give it a try. If I don't like it, I'll quickly withdraw and go to medical school, since it starts a few weeks later." But the thought of denying someone else a place in medical school by my holding on to an acceptance forced the decision; it was for seminary, which I entered thinking it was just another form of graduate school—for the ministry rather than medicine. The sight of women working as doctors and my parents serving as active laypeople in the church had "blinded" me to any identity crisis raised by such scriptural admonitions as 1 Timothy 2:11–15. For me, the pull toward the ordained ministry was a "call."

MOTIVATION FOR MINISTRY

It was not until I was ordained and serving as a pastor that I had to work out my answer to those who tried to silence me with their quoting of scripture. And my first response was to dismiss disapproval with, "Why would I have gone through such a crisis in choosing a vocation if I wasn't intended to be a pastor? There must be other interpretations for the verses you cite." It was then that I began to read every biblical reference for and against women serving as clergy, studying them from both the historical and the cultural perspective but finding the most insightful pursuit to be the biographies in both the Old and New Testaments. In those personalities I saw a two-level attitude toward women; in general, it was society's no to their being anything more than a man's possession, in individual situations it was yes to a woman's God-given talent that God invited her to offer for God's use, with Mary's "Magnificat" being the poetic verbalization of one woman's response. In specific people, women of the Bible (the same Bible that labeled women "from man" and charged them to be silent in the teaching of religion) I saw individuals—women—serving God as judge, prophet, deaconess, pastor, bishop. I had to admit, not all negative references could be explained away with a thorough exegesis of the text, but for me, those references took second place to the individuals whose lives were a contradiction to those verses. I took that apparent contradiction to be an invitation for a Christian to engage in the struggle to overcome gender discrimination, realizing that that is an inequality as intolerable and as un-Christian as slavery. But if our elimination of slavery is an example of how long it will take us in this venture, then a woman struggling to be identified as a clergyperson is just entering the dawning of that fray. That is why I see a woman's ability to identify herself as one whose ministry is acceptable to God and ordained by God as an essential step. Then she can give second place to Bible verses quoted to deny her that ministry and first place to her response to God's call to service, which leads to another exploration prompted by the word identity: a woman's identification of her reason for becoming a minister (an inclusive investigation, for a man should pursue the same inquiry). Reading scriptural biographies, one sees that God does call women as well as men into God-ordained service, a frustrating fact for women whose church does not acknowledge the biography of her "call"! It is a fact that shapes some clergywomen's practice of ministry.

At the April 16, 1985 Alumni Convocation of the Lutheran Seminary in Philadelphia, Martin E. Marty was asked by a clergywoman how a church can be moved to accept women as pastors. First, he reminded the questioner that the church throughout history has not welcomed anything new, and so, he counseled, "as a Christian, be patient." His response only fired the impatience of the inquirer, but she did keep her dissatisfaction veiled under a cool "Thank you!" At that moment she decided to refrain from identifying herself as a pastor with a mission to champion reform, advocate for change, and display a holy impatience against all prejudices that dehumanize anyone, including women wanting to be clergy.

A woman working for a doctor of theology degree in a Canadian seminary of the Anglican Church also teaches seminarians, women and men. Her observation is that the younger the women, the more impatient they are. Their motivation for ministry is definitely to be champion, advocate, protester. Their mission will be to eliminate exclusiveness in the language of theology and worship, and to level the hierarchy that is seen as a distortion of church polity. They will work to demolish ecclesiastical structures, for those structures are a hindrance to and a corruption of the gospel these women are called to preach.

Research from U.S. seminaries and churches, reported in *Women of the Cloth,* suggests that some women are tending to seek ordination for another reason, not to change the church through their ministry, but to go to a seminary that will equip them to be competent. Older women tend to be first-career homemakers, lay leaders in their church, trained volunteers in the community, who choose the ministry as their new, midlife-change career. Their experience has been one of involvement in systems and structures; their purpose is to improve the agendas and organizations they have known by acquiring the qualifications to be proficient clergy. Their commitment to change will be only those changes that will improve the institutional church and make existing congregations more responsive to the mission the gospel calls them to carry into the world.

There is a third group, whose sole motivation for ministry is the oldest—a call from God. Ordination is sought to perform tasks perceived to be given by God, including miserable housing, inadequate salary, and a parish too small for a full-time pastor—unless the pastor is a woman, which suggests why abandoned churches welcome a clergywoman. She'll go where a man would not think of going. Her "call" is her entrance into the ministry even if the location of ministry demeans that call—which is a caldron of internal conflict kept cool only as long as the woman does not scrutinize the route she has had to take to legitimate her ordination. However, a parish shunned by others as an insult to a call to ministry may prove to be a church waiting to be pastored into life. Because most of our nation's congregations are under 200 adults in their count of active members, they may be the places where a strong sense of "call" will prove to be a positive motivation to ministry for woman or man. Such places may also prove to be the congregations in which pastors enjoy the privilege of being the clergy who discover and nurture the vitality of a small congregation, proving that Jackson W. Carroll could edit a book and give it the title *Small Churches Are Beautiful* and David R. Ray could write an entire book called *Small Churches Are the Right Size*.

"Identity" is the word that centers in the individual, woman or man, who is a clergyperson. What is her or his motivation for ministry? How are the scriptures used to affirm or negate that identification? For another person's perception: "You look just like . . . ," implying no individuality among clergywomen, or an inequality in the form of address of a clergyperson, withholding some titles from a woman while using them for a man, may be only a response to or a mirroring of a pastor's blurred identity. That is a lesson I have learned in the classroom of the parish: if scripture's biographies legitimate a woman's call to ministry, then a clergywoman mirrors that call. She, not others, is the primary reference for her identity as an individual who is a clergyperson. There are, however, qualifications and realities that complement or hinder the legitimacy of that identification. Another lesson and so another chapter.

3 • REALITIES

The Classroom

On two occasions, May 23, 1962 and June 19, 1967, a very active laywoman, who was also supportive of her pastor, enjoyed going to the local post office to make an announcement introduced with a question. "Guess what our pastor just did?" When she had the full attention of postmaster and everyone else turning the dial to open his or her mailbox, she beamed and said, "Our pastor's had a baby!" It was as though she was answering the riddle of the century, which only members of her church could solve; for all others it would remain a riddle until they begged her for an explanation, which she was baiting them to seek. Then she answered, "Our pastor is a woman!"

The Lesson

In that woman's baitlike answer I saw one of many lessons a clergywoman learns in the continuing education curriculum of the parish ministry. These are the old, traditional "classrooms" in which clergymen as well as clergywomen must sit and struggle to learn how to balance ministry, marriage, family. There are also new ones for which no lesson plans have been written. Clergy are creating the curriculum by being both the source of the studies and the student. At the same time, women find that the subjects do place more requirements on them than on men, beginning with ministry, marriage, and family.

Just as I started my ministry I looked forward to the birth of our first child, and only a week before heading for the hospital asked, "How is this going to work out, being a minister and a mother?"

While in high school I had worked during the summer and on weekends and holidays in a hospital maternity ward. Because my aunt was the supervisor of the department and I was premed, I was trained to do what today would be the work of a licensed practical nurse, including working in the labor and delivery rooms. Labor pains and birth were, therefore, everyday occurrences; I'd go through them too! That was my reasoning as I faced the birth of our first child, no apprehension about labor, only the impatience of waiting. But even the waiting was made easy. A clergyman serving as a school's chaplain needed a place to preach so pastoral search committees could "look at him." He did not want his desire to return to the parish ministry to be obvious. It was an ideal situation. He'd cover for the four Sundays I'd be away, beginning when called; the circumstances were a perfect cover for his intentions. He was called to serve the church whose committee came to hear him while he was serving as a "vacation supply." And I also found a way to have a four-Sunday, four-week vacation. Usually it was three. After having two children, I asked if there wasn't another way to get a month's vacation. The trustees answered, "Be here ten years." I stayed almost fourteen.

Incidentally, when our second son was born on a Monday morning, the event intrigued James E. Wagner—retired co-president of the United Church of Christ and editor of the (UCC) Pennsylvania Southeast Conference's newspaper—so much that he wrote an article announcing the arrival under the title "Twenty-four Hours After the Benediction!"

Even more entertaining for me was the fact that a robe was a good cover. Both times when my husband and I were anticipating our sons' arrivals worshipers greeted me at the door saying, "Have a nice vacation!" not knowing what kind of a "vacation" it was going to be! The real surprise was mine, not theirs. I had not thought much beyond birth! And so, after the humorous send-off on "a nice vacation" and the hearing of "It's a boy!" there was the shock, "What now? How was I going to respond to this reality?"

MINISTRY AND MOTHERHOOD

There were three answers. One was my husband's response to my desperate question raised a week before Jonathan arrived: "How is this going to work out?" To which Howard replied, "Don't worry, Martha. We'll work everything out together!" And we have. From the very first hours at home with a new baby, my husband has been as much of a parent, and many times more of a parent, than I have, and therefore, he has been my best teacher, showing me that marriage and ministry are possible and even preferable. I did not appreciate the combination of home and church all at once. To be honest, I needed ten more years and a call that took me from a parish to a regional staff position to give Howard's answer—especially his word together—a religious significance.

One of my new assignments was social concerns, and that assignment brought me into contact with Roman Catholic orders in Philadelphia. One nun who carried major responsibilities for the Cardinal's Commission on Racial Justice in Philadelphia impressed me. She did not wear a habit, the garb of her order, but she did live with other sisters of her religious community. There, life wasn't much different from life in our house. Each had chores to do, and prayer was much like our attempts at family devotions. Later a friend studying for the priesthood gave us an inside understanding of life in the mother house of his community. Male or female, priest or nun, life in the houses of the orders they chose to be their family made me see the religious significance of our home and family. We were and are a community of the "religious," and our home is our "mother house." We are to one another in our family what sisters or priests are in their order. And like an order, we are open to welcoming others into our "community"—some on a part-time basis, others long-term. Some come for a short visit, others come to work. My parents, for example, when our children were infants and preschoolers, came every weekend to take over the household chores. There was also an on-call neighbor who served as an unpaid "nanny." And then there was a high school student, a young woman who later entered the ministry and went on to combine pastoring and parenting. I like to think she was nurtured for that service in part through her time spent in our "community."

In the New Testament's words, we are "a church in our home." Ministry begins in our ministry to one another. That was a profound thought to which I was introduced by a Roman Catholic sister and a priest who do not know what they taught me when they talked about their religious community. It is a lesson Howard started and they completed and our family is still working at learning and living. A lifelong pursuit!

A second answer to my "How is this going to work out, being a minister and mother?" was the enthusiasm of the congregation. They had waited for this moment for twenty-five years. And the house now serving as a parsonage had never been the home for a family; its builders were childless, their impressive monument to their wealth, complete with tile roof imported from Sri Lanka (then Ceylon), was bought by the church when their estate was settled. Then the second floor became the parsonage-apartment for a bachelor pastor while the first floor was used as meeting space. We were the first to live in the whole house, turn on all the lights, and try to furnish all the rooms and curtain its ninety-six windows! We were also the first to have children who would scratch the inlaid hardwood floors, break the irreplaceable beveled glass in the doors, and enjoy rooms large enough to be indoor playgrounds. The congregation welcomed all that was to come with the coming of our sons, Jonathan and David. They looked at our life in the parsonage to be a "building program" they had waited more than a generation to celebrate. Their joy-filled response taught me that nothing improves a pastor's relation with her or his church family as much as an addition to the clergy's family. That was the second answer that allayed my apprehension—except for the times when our children said "something cute" (a parishioner's evaluation; "something embarrassing" to Howard and me). There was the time our two-year-old Jonathan started a conversation with a woman, "Do you know why———(the woman's daughter-in-law) isn't cleaning for us anymore?" Without waiting for an answer, he said, "She left too much dust around!" Of course, many ears heard this and many mouths broadcast the report! Jon redeemed himself and us when, at the same age, he blurted out a question in Pennsylvania German, the language of conversation among older members. They were impressed but also apprehensive. How much *did* he understand? And if he knew what they were saying in Pennsylvania German, how much did he carry home?

A third answer that dispelled my apprehension over being both minister and mother was the history of the congregation's and the community's families. They had been farmers and, in this generation, were changing to factory workers, both women and men. But one detail in their lives did not change. They still went about their chores as they had on the farm; everyone had a job, and there were at least three generations in a household, or living close enough to work together. Grandmother babysat while Mother worked in the pants factory; Father shopped for the weekly groceries while Mother did the laundry; and Friday night was the time for the whole family to eat out, walk the malls, or "do" the town's stores. As I watched them I chuckled over the adage "Woman's place is in the home." That quip would have insulted the man who came home from work before his wife and prided himself on being the chef of the family and regularly prepared the evening meal. And that quote would have gotten a laugh out of the woman who knew that her factory work was probably less demanding on her time than her grandmother's life on the farm—where women always worked "outside the home."

In the 1970s, when I was researching family life in the colonial period, I read Stevenson W. Fletcher's *Pennsylvania Agriculture Country Life 1646–1840* and realized that Pennsylvania German wives worked with their husbands in the field. This sight horrified a visitor from New England in 1810; she remarked that in her colony, woman's

30

place was in the home. If her Pennsylvania hostess only worked there, she would have wondered what to do with all her extra time!

There was another precedent that I was reluctant to enjoy. The parsonage family of an earlier generation had always employed young women of the congregation as maids and aides. These young women were now the older members, who wistfully recalled the honor they had had. Our family did not see that service to be an "honor," and so we shunned the apparent willingness to clean, do laundry, iron clothes, babysit, until I realized that I was denying them a service because of my guilt. I had a problem—the self-indictment of being totally responsible, and therefore totally answerable, for every speck of dust, every dish, every piece of laundry, and every serving of food. That obsession did not rule me as a child; my mother, in exasperation, would continually exclaim, "How can you sit and look at work?" (work being dust, dishes, etc.). I could and I did— until our home became a parsonage. Then I changed to a self-assigned sentence of guilt and was impossible to live with. I resented being robbed of time to do the work of a pastor because I had to do the work of a homemaker. And not to do the work of a homemaker would imply I was open season for any critic who wanted to take a shot at dust, dirty dishes, unfolded laundry, and any other evidence of a slovenly housekeeper of "their" house. It was a Catch-22 before the word was used!

Sheer exhaustion forced a change, or was it my academic training overcoming my guilt? I turned to thinking mathe-matically: "I am only one member of four in this house-hold; therefore, I only contribute to twenty-five percent of the dust, dishes, etc. That means I should bear only one fourth of the responsibilities. To take on more is to 'deprive' my family of assuming their share." The thought of being a "mother house," a religious community, gave my mathematical reasoning a theological firmness. Now we share the guilt of dust, dishes, and laundry; oh, yes, laundry. That is the one chore that never nears completion. Sometimes our urge to fill our dining table with guests (our table seats twelve) is the pressure it creates to clear the table of unfolded laundry! Just last week, when in an hour the house was turned from a shambles into sparkling clean rooms with everything in place, Howard remarked, "It's amazing what we accomplish. It's almost unbelievable!" Now we share in the chores so we may all rejoice in the results. My release from guilt cannot, however, be attributed to my mathematical reasoning. When I traced my freedom to its real source, I realized that it came from the heritage of an agricultural community in which everyone worked on the farm, and a congregation in which members felt that it was a privilege to work for the parsonage family. We offered that "privilege" to several members when I learned to put aside my problem. Incidentally, I can again "look at work" when it is dust, laundry, etc, and not see it. There are too many more important and more satisfying activities—like being a pastor.

Another learning is that moving to our own home was veiled wisdom. At the time, changing from a parish to the Conference staff, from a parsonage to our own property, seemed like a cruel requirement. The only house we could afford lost one wall in a hurricane a week after the sale; for months we had to live with a hand pump out front and an outhouse out back, which, in the winter, our son Jon called the "Frosty Maid." He was so right! When I tried to heat it with a kerosene lamp, I almost caused a fire. But now our home is four walls and much more. It is a love-filled dwelling restored by our family, my parents, church members—and a plumber whose church prohibited him from working on a Sunday. After church he came and nodded directions as Howard put the heating system together. Looking back, the forced move was not cruel; it was an "opportunity" to learn that it is appropriate for pastors (as well as parishioners) to maintain their own residence. Such an arrangement also relieves a congregation of worrying over what the pastor and family may be doing to "the church's home"!

DIVORCE

These learnings are "traditional realities." There is another issue that isn't new to families, but it is new to a clergy household. Divorce. Past generations offered two options: (1) A pastor "left the ministry" or a teaching place was found in a college or a seminary, where he (and past generations' divorced clergy were men) was removed from the judgment of a congregation. (2) If the pastor was deemed "the innocent party," he could continue in a local church. Today ministers may simply move on to another pastorate after a divorce. Attitudes are changing. Is it because the statistics of divorce are increasing and clergy are not exempt, or because congregations and judicatories are becoming more human, more honest—admitting that clergy marriages carry no guarantee of "being made in heaven"?

During my years on the Conference staff I agonized with a clergy couple as they faced the realities of conflicts that could not be resolved. One spouse faced his sexual orientation. He had thought marriage would be the answer. It wasn't. Nor could counseling, prayer, scripture make him a heterosexual. I felt the couple's pain, but I also celebrated their honesty and their freedom to let each be the individual he or she was. I also witnessed another marriage end in divorce and the clergyperson remarry—and move to a new parish far enough away from the first to be out of earshot of comments but never free from the biographical detail, "You know this is his second wife? He's divorced!" But the details leading up to that report were never included. The couple had met before the husband planned to study for the ministry. Before his decision, they had not lived by their marriage vows; each gave the other permission to "love freely." And each did. Then the husband began to think about religion and the Christian faith. His decision to become a Christian and to study for the ministry prompted his struggle to commit himself to his wife; no more loving freely. She was not ready to make the same choice. For him, that forced another decision: ministry *or* marriage. The two were incompatible. He chose the ministry. He agonized over Christ's words (Mark 10:1–12) about divorce as a clergywoman agonizes over Paul's words about silence in the church (1 Corinthians 14:34 and 1 Timothy 2:11–13). Divorce, the same as gender, must not be used to deny people the opportunity of ministry.

In a divorce a minister, male or female, may hear a church say, "Society does it, but you can't. You're different because the scripture says . . . , and you must live according to scripture." The words quoted are even more imposing than Paul's, for the speaker is Christ. And in the case of a divorced woman, a church's approval of her ordination may be a closed door, locked and barred. The lock, Paul's words; the bar, Christ's!

I wonder if the uneven attitudes toward clergy and divorce will ever be resolved for the clergy. My learning is a feeling for the agony of those in the ministry who try to resolve being divorced by reasoning that their call is greater than the scripture verses some would use to deny them that calling.

34

CLERGY COUPLES

When the clergyperson is a married woman, other realities may threaten her marriage, her ministry, or both. If her spouse also is a minister, where are they going to serve? Will the woman experience a blatant or subtle silencing by her church as she is forced to take the church no one else wants while her husband pastors a much more viable congregation? Or will she be forced to find other work because "we just can't locate a church for you as well as your husband." Denominations' statistics prove the questions are not supposition, but fact.

When *Wall Street Journal* writer Linda M. Watkins interviewed Joan and Fred Hamlin, a Methodist clergy couple (December 24, 1986), she reported a story that is not atypical. The wife serves two congregations, of 25 and 70; her husband's church has 164 members. His wife's assignment prompts Fred to say, "I hurt for her."

I carry a hurt. It is the pain of the thought that my husband, a clergyperson, may be a teacher today not only because he is an excellent teacher, but also because he is sensitive to protecting our marriage and our family from the realities that threaten a clergy couple. Perhaps his "hurt" for me, more than his preference for teaching, prompted his decision to teach, making it more of a sacrifice than a choice. My clergy spouse is my personal experience of loving vicariously; he tempers his ministry to enable mine. Because experience has equipped me to believe that a congregation will find it difficult to "see double," to accept two rather than one, and will compare "him" with "her" (with a multiplicity of tensions generated by that comparison), I am cautious about clergy couples in shared ministries and

35

copastorates. They demand an ego strength—or is it a martyr's constitution?—which I know I did not have at the beginning of our ministry, and I would not like to test my capability now! This is another learning that began as and remains my confession. It prompts another confession: my admiration for couples who are the positive examples.

Denominations do have stories to tell of clergy couples who are proving that congregations can be served by pastors who are husband and wife. One is told through Jim and Marie Jerge, Lutheran pastors of three congregations in Dunkirk, New York, featured in their seminary's bulletin *P.S.* (Philadelphia's Lutheran Seminary, Volume 69, Number 3). Theirs is an arrangement of carefully calculated time and responsibilities: "Jim is full-time at Grace, Marie half-time at St. Mark, and together they serve Zion—Marie half time and Jim 10%." A total of 110 percent—which is the mathematics of the ministry! When asked to talk about a clergy couple's problems, Marie and Jim do not answer with illustrations of discrimination but of personal frustration. Their response is "time." Not enough time "to do their work, to be together, and schedules that are totally different." Perhaps their response is free of more negative references because they began their ministries with an agreed-upon decision "never to speak for the other" and "not to talk shop all the time." Marie's comments are:

Each as pastor fully understands the other's commitment to the job, something people and spouses who are not clergy often have difficulty understanding. For the commitment is much more than a job—it is rather one's life. What being a clergy couple does is allow us to understand that mental attitude. We can share our job with a sense of understanding and a bit of sensitivity to each other. Our commitment to the Church and to Jesus Christ is the number one cornerstone of our marriage.

I read and reread their words and want to know more.

What are the people in their parishes like? Why are they receptive to the Jerges' ministry, and why do they support and encourage their pastors? Why are the Jerges' experiences as a clergy couple positive, while the experiences of others are negative and even destructive of a ministry and sometimes a marriage? Marie and Jim Jerge are my teachers on this new reality of the ministry called "clergy couples."

NONCLERGY SPOUSE

Another reality is the woman pastor whose husband does not share her vocation. Placement can be a real chore and threat to a marriage, and relocation of the nonclergy spouse or the pastor's desire to move on to another church may make a move impossible. One of my classmates in seminary went from a pastorate to marriage to unemployment. In the past twenty years she has held temporary positions as a part-time director of Christian education in churches of other denominations. Now, twenty-seven years after ordination, she is a pastor again. Her parish is her neighborhood, where she has found enough members to call her to be their pastor.

The clergywoman I quoted in chapter 2 reports that *the* obstacle to a woman's positive experience in the parish ministry is "being married to a nonclergy spouse. When she wants to move she has a problem." I watch women caught in that trap and see what happens when it is unresolved; there can be tensions in a marriage, and in a pastorate, and there is the threat of destroying a clergywoman's love for the church she committed her life to serve. How can she honor an institution that is threatening her marriage and denying her employment?

More questions! When will the church count among its unemployed clergy the ordained women married to non-clergy spouses? Will we encourage them, like my seminary classmate, to go out and create a ministry? When they do, will we accept and celebrate their initiative and the results? Will congregations and judicatories put them to work? There is more to do than any one pastor can handle, even in the smallest church; will they be invited to be part of the action and be recognized and compensated for their service? I feel the pain of those who are suffering and will suffer until the rest of us in the church, the employed, hurt enough to remove them from the church's unpublished list of unemployed clergy! Theirs is a lesson for which the lesson plans are still waiting to be written.

SEXUAL HARASSMENT

I had to read it in an article in *The Observer*, monthly magazine of the United Church of Canada, to realize how prevalent and destructive sexual harassment is. The lines I read prompted me to write for the full report that the short article quoted. A committee of the denomination's Division of Ministry Personnel and Education has responded with examples, counsel for victims, guidelines for employers and churches, literature, and addresses of Canada's Human Rights Commission. But of all the information, that which gave impetus to the project was a 1983 survey response. Thirty-five percent of the 238 women indicated that they had been the victim of sexual harassment as a theological student or in a job as a woman in professional ministry.

A 1986 survey of 138 ordained women in the United Church of Christ yielded a response of 43 percent. Another "reality"! Another lesson for me: *The Observer* (March

1986, p. 28) quoted an Episcopalian priest, Patricia Park, as telling women seminarians the reason for their being unacceptable in the ministry. As women, they "raise issues of sex and religion, (they) challenge the latent body-spirit dualism within Christianity. Images of women may be used to sell liquor, cars and cigars, but not Jesus." According to clergywomen in the United Church of Canada, they not only have fifty years of ordained ministry to celebrate; they also have the price of their gender to document—from remarks and jokes, to pornographic pictures, to gestures and sexual advances, to physical assault. The 1986 policy statement approved by the General Council Executive of the United Church of Canada tells a sampling of stories to illustrate data. A teenager refused to go to the youth group and to church because the thirty-year-old married male minister was "behaving inappropriately." A church secretary was harassed by a layman who tried to force her into accepting his "friendship" by threatening to tell everyone she was "involved" with the pastor. A woman seminarian serving an internship to gain pastoral experience requested the pastor not to refer to her as "his nice little helper" who was really "looking for a man." She was labeled a young woman with "sexual problems" and therefore in need of counseling. And there was "Gail—Clergywoman":

GAIL—CLERGYWOMAN

I had been on the pastoral charge for seven months and it was my first annual meeting. I was feeling good about the amount of work I had accomplished and how I had settled in and seemingly been accepted by the community. At the meeting the chairperson of the board publicly stated that although most people seemed pleased with their first woman minister that he had heard several people were not happy and felt I was not doing enough work. I was devastated and humiliated.

A week later we were travelling to Presbytery together and I asked him what he meant at the meeting. He laughed and said he could resolve the problem if I wanted him to do that. When I questioned him further, he suggested that we could stop at a neighboring town on our way home from Presbytery that evening for further "conversation." I was so naive that I asked why we couldn't talk now. "Oh come on . . ." he said, "women are not made to be ministers. Tonight I'll show you what women are really for. We can have a bit of a good time." I couldn't believe my ears and told him so. He looked at me and said, "If you want to have a chance while you are in our pastoral charge you'll spend more than one evening alone with me. Otherwise you'll be gone before another annual meeting." (*Sexual Harassment in the Church*, The United Church of Canada, 1986, p. 8).

I must admit, when I give thought to sexual harassment, I could go on a personal search and come up with stories, but I do not have them as a ready reference because I have unconsciously accepted the "myths" identified by the United Church of Canada. I must now unlearn them and accept the realities. Many women are affected, not a few; it happens in seminaries and churches as well as in industry and business; it doesn't go away; a woman does not "ask for it"; when charges are made, the woman will be ridiculed, mistreated, charged, not believed and supported; because what she calls "sexual harassment" may be excused as "a fact of life."

So what does a woman do? A clergywoman whose job may depend on her keeping quiet, going along, and being victimized by her sexuality—how does she handle such exploitation?

My first learning is that sexual harassment is as the United Church of Canada identifies it: "a sin" and "a violation of the integrity of persons based on unequal power relationships and usually on gender" *(Sexual Harassment in the Church)*. But the steps to call harassment a violation are far more complex and, I fear, far from a uniform process for a victim to follow. In some churches there is no policy statement other than, "Well, that's why you shouldn't be in the ministry. You are a temptress of men!" Myths die hard, especially when they feed sexual appetites and commercial enterprises, as Patricia Park has observed: women, made "to sell liquor, cars, and cigars, but not Jesus!" I have no hope for women in such churches, and if asked, my counsel to them would be "Get out! Find another church!"

In churches that have policy statements there is the next chore: to follow policy with procedure. Is there a committee to whom incidents of sexual harassment are reported? Is there a form for documenting the charge? Are there suggested steps leading to a formal charge—others with similar experiences, witnesses to the victim's harassment, a supportive person? That is the most important detail for me—someone who will be the victim's counselor and advocate, a person who believes in her and stands with her. I now sense that that role may be my unfilled calling to other clergywomen and the most unmet need in collegiality among women ministers.

In the next chapter this reality is expanded from clergy to congregation, the subject of sexual harassment as practiced by individuals in the parish who live by the myths, and women who are the victims of those myths, and a woman pastor's response to both. In this chapter I would like to combine sexual harassment of clergywomen with a practical—and controversial—issue: how the clergy dress when doing the work of the church.

CLERGY GARB

When women were first ordained in the Scandinavian churches, I followed with interest the reports of a suitable dress being designed for the soon-to-be female pastors. The event made headline news, and feature stories gave full coverage to the new fashion. If the same subject were to be an issue today, I would no longer be interested; I would be irritated. My point of view has changed. I now see the subject of how to dress a Scandinavian clergywoman as one more example that a woman supposedly accepted for service in the church is really not quite acceptable. Evidence: the need for a garb designed for a woman.

Arguments that urge "But women shouldn't dress in men's apparel—it's too masculine; a woman should not lose her femininity" turn me into a crusader committed to "re-dressing" the clergy, not in new apparel, but in a correct understanding of the office of the ministry (the subject of chapter 6). Here my "crusading" is confined to clergy garb and to comments that expand the discussion of clergy apparel from a matter of identity to an issue of harassment. If the "office" of ministry called "pastor" is a role, a function, with a garb, that garb should be worn by both women and men ordained to the ministry. The dress should be the same for both genders. That is my argument and my learning, which was taught to me by a missionary of our denomination, the Rev. Anna Dederer.

Anna is from Germany, served in Micronesia, and came to the United Church of Christ by way of the U.S. Navy and her need to become a citizen of the United States if she wanted to return to her "people" in the South Pacific. Because Anna made that choice she became our friend, as a missionary aided by the congregation my husband and I served. Anna visited us whenever she was on furlough. How different her background was—a woman raised in pre-World War II Germany and a Lutheran parish where she was working as an assistant to the pastor, preparing for mission service, where she would do the pastoral ministry she was not permitted to do at home. One more detail is important (my introduction to a lesson on "clergy garb"). In the islands there was no such thing as dressing for the office of ministry. The natives wore as little clothing as possible; it was too hot. Anna's "garb" was a lightweight housedress. Anna, therefore, had no inclination toward ministerial garb; it was totally impractical in the islands, and in Germany clergy vestments were worn only by men, since there were no women pastors.

One day while Anna was on furlough, we planned to attend a church service together. While she waited for me to come downstairs, she talked with my mother. I walked into the room, ready to leave, but not in a hurry. I wanted them to finish their conversation. Anna, however, interrupted it as she turned, moved toward me, put her hands on my arms, to cause me to stop in place, and said, "Now, you look like a pastor!" Her German-English inflection gave those words a dignity I do not want to forget. Anna was announcing that my dress—a suit with a clerical collar (at that time it was the traditional black vest with the step collar holding a white celluloid collar)—was not a suit reserved for the all-male clergy in her parish in Germany; it was the garb of the office of the ordained clergy, the garb for a woman as well as a man.

Anna's announcement was my lesson on a practical approach to reducing sexual harassment: wear the garb of the office!—counsel with which to take issue, I know. There is the argument that the garb is too tainted with the male image of clergy, and therefore a garb demeaning to a woman, as though in assuming the traditional vestments, a woman is giving her assent to all the harassment that would deny her the office of pastor. There is also the contention that clergy should not be set apart, and garb must be the first mark of separation to be abandoned. I would contest each argument and counter each with Anna's words, "Now, you look like a pastor!" To wear the garb of the office is to be a representative of the ministry of that office, and to model that garb as the dress of anyone ordained to the ministry. That, to me, is a practical detail in addressing sexual harassment.

Motherhood, divorce, clergy couples, nonclergy spouse, sexual harassment. Some would cite these as the rationale to deny ordination to women, and for some clergywomen these are unresolved problems that deny them a place in the ministry. These women are my teachers; their personal crises are illustrations of James Russell Lowell's lines:

> New occasions teach new duties,
> Time makes ancient good uncouth;
> They must upward still and onward,
> Who would keep abreast of truth.

Aren't the problems named in this chapter our "new occasions" to face the "truth" of our humanness and our sexuality?

I'd like to believe that clergywomen can turn these "realities" into "occasions" to teach church and society to be honest, admitting that clergy and laity, Christian and non-Christian, are plagued by the same problems. I'd like to hope that women ministers, working through those problems, will be honored as "teachers," not rejected as pastors.

4 • ACCEPTABILITY

The Classroom

The first week in our first parish I enthusiastically responded to a phone call. "Sure, I'd be glad to baptize a church member's baby." After a visit with the couple the time for baptism was scheduled for the next Sunday, during the church service.

The next week there was a similar call; another baby, another baptism on the next Sunday.

After two Sundays and two baptisms a member of the Diaconate called me aside and said, "We don't do that here!"

"Do what?" I asked.

"Baptize *infants.*"

"What's wrong with that? The church records show that there have been baptisms of infants as well as adults."

"Yes," said the Diaconate member, "but infants have always been baptized in the back room, not in church during a service."

I asked to hear more and was told that "back room baptisms" were a concession made to members of the congregation who came from churches that practiced infant baptism. The church's practice was baptism by sprinkling after catechetical instruction.

That quick lesson in a church's history and theology became another classroom with a full curriculum on the subject of how to be accepted as pastor.

The Lesson

"Acceptability" may involve a formal study of statistics, such as census tracts and textbooks on the sociology of religion. They are good starter-resources. But they are only the general introduction to learning about a community that will be both a pastor's parish and her or his home. How does a pastor move from the printed page to firsthand data? What are the "readings" to note, the real statistics and sociological data that describe a community and a congregation? What are the unwritten subtleties that will determine whether or not a clergyperson will be accepted?

That question may be a point to protest, or at least challenge as a legitimate inquiry. The challenge may be that I am making a false assumption, that a community and congregation have a "personality." The protest may be that a pastor should resist being influenced by a community or, even worse, fitting into a mold (a protest with biblical backing, Romans 12:2). My protest is that a pastor being accepted by a community and a congregation is not a question of conformity, but of knowledge, of taking the time to determine if either or both have a "personality." Maybe there is none, but I find that assessment to be a remote condition. Years as a member of a Conference staff reinforce my protest.

My responsibilities took me from two urban centers, to economically depressed towns, to rural areas unchanged from the days when they were first settled more than two hundred years ago. Each place had its uniqueness that, when observed, was a composite of its "personality." And in urban areas I saw a complex of characteristics. Move one block away and neighbors consider you no longer part of their community, no longer in the "neighborhood." The churches reflected the same attitude. Together, community and congregation proved that each definitely had its own personality.

KNOWING THE COMMUNITY

In Reading, Pennsylvania there was a Cuban congregation housed in large church facilities. The congregation welcomed the Spanish-speaking Christians who had recently escaped when Fidel Castro came into power. By the early 1970s most of the Cubans had found high-salaried jobs and moved into the suburbs, where they affiliated with churches near their new homes. The Spanish-speaking pastor needed a congregation and the neighborhood around the church appeared to be filled with prospects. They, too, spoke Spanish. But the pastor politely turned down the invitation to visit in the neighborhood and went on to teach in a college. The Conference committee could not understand his move. He had to tell us only after our insistence that he and his congregation were Cubans; the new neighbors around the church were Puerto Ricans. "So?" we questioned, still not able to understand what he was trying to tell us without having to say more. He had to go into detail, explaining that there are six types of Spanish-speaking people, vastly different from one another economically, socially, culturally. He was of one group, and "they" (the Puerto Ricans) were of another. That was the early 1970s. Now the Puerto Ricans are moving, not by choice, but because of urban "renewal." In less than thirty years one neighborhood has undergone three changes, each ethnically different from the other, moving from middle-class families, to poverty level and unemployed field laborers, to prime land for commercial development. In a congregation's time that area has had three very different histories, and each history has had an influence on its pastors and their acceptability.

During my first year on Conference staff I traveled from Reading to walk the streets in North Philadelphia. It was a warm spring day. A black laywoman from a neighborhood church was my hostess. I said to her, "I lived not too many blocks from here in my high school days when I attended Girls' High School. How many girls from this neighborhood go to Girls' High now?" She ignored my question and turned the conversation to another subject. Later our Minister of Metropolitan Mission invited me to walk toward the local school. It was 1:30 in the afternoon and the noise coming from the open windows was deafening. Peeking through one window I saw the disorder of the junior high students left to "entertain" themselves through the day while the teacher sat reading the newspaper! Then the Metropolitan Minister explained, "Martha, you asked how many students go on to Girls' High. Girls in this school would never qualify; they don't even get a good elementary education." The explanation had to be expanded to the politics of the situation, a neighborhood school with teachers who came in to sit at their desks and then went to homes far distant from that school—not by choice, but by placement, while the teachers from the neighborhood were assigned outside their neighborhood. All of which was intentional: to keep a neighborhood's students from being upwardly mobile. The embarrassment I had felt after asking my question changed to anger that children were being deprived of an education. Then I thought to myself, "I lived a few blocks from those streets and never knew what was happening in a nearby neighborhood."

I began my days on the Conference staff dismissing my first days in the ministry that began with that Diaconate member's protest, "We don't do that here! Baptize infants!" I had to learn all over again that a community's history cannot be ignored. But learning that history is a lesson in itself. Books are a good resource; people are better. People in the community's stores, restaurants, post office; people met on the street waiting for the bus or the light; people waiting in the doctor's office; people met walking the streets or being wherever the community's people gather. For me, in the first parish, the places were the post office, the local newspaper desk, and a family restaurant. And wherever I went I asked, "How long have you lived here?" Some were their family's seventh generation recently moved to town from the farmland cleared in the 1730s. They had seven generations of personal history to tell. As they told their stories, I saw acceptance happening. Their community became mine, and by their choice, they welcomed me as a neighbor because I valued their neighborhood's history.

An area's history is not the only lesson. There is also a social code, which is a subtle test of a pastor's acceptability. After learning that code, a pastor must decide how much "acceptability" he or she wants to attain. Every Friday night the local firehouse was *the* place to eat for everyone except the pastor. "Pastors don't go there" was the word. "Why?" The explanation, "Because there's a bar." Should that explanation become an issue? When a community has a double standard—one for clergy, another for the rest of the community—what "codes" are worth protesting? When is a protest that threatens acceptance inept and unneighborly? That is a critical question when the pastor is a woman. Her acceptability may depend on how well she complies with a community's social code. A reason to learn about the community and then wrestle with what has been learned. It is a wrestling I consider too important to ignore or dismiss. I also know it is a concession a clergywoman may protest as one more "put down." But is it? Or is a woman pastor who takes issue with a community's expectations for the clergy denying the community its way of identifying a clergyperson whom they consider "acceptable"? Personally I would rather chuckle to myself over a community's double standards and play the clergy code role, accepting it as another learning about acceptability.

KNOWING THE CONGREGATION

Because a pastor is called by a congregation, not a community, there are more learnings and more references to check than the profile a church prepared when searching for a pastor. One learning is a congregation's history studied through several sources: written histories, newspaper articles, and casual conversations with neighbors, beginning with a request for directions to the church. Responses may be "What church are you looking for? Never heard of it!" "Oh, yes, that's the building with peeling paint and uncut grass!" or "That's a fine church, I'm not a member but many of my friends are." How revealing a community's comments may be!

Another pursuit is a study of the church's theology—not

the one taught in the catechetical material (if there is any—a detail worth noting), but the one evident in its order of service, its church school curriculum, its events such as country "Gospel" singers, organ recitals, cantatas, or church suppers. What does the congregation do when it's "putting on a program"? And with all the observations, like noting entries in the church record, there may be learnings that come only after practicing what is taken to be the church's theology and then finding that there are unwritten details, like "back room baptisms"! When criticism and reaction indicate that there is more to learn than the records indicate, how does a pastor respond? Another critical question with another debatable answer.

My response, taught in the classroom of the parish, was from that moment of "We don't do that here!" to learn what was the thing to "do here." I began asking for information and then invited the church's official board to review how that practice came into being and how to conduct a service of baptism in a manner that expressed the word sacrament. They continued to teach me as I listened to theology yield to church politics. "We can't insist on baptizing only adults because we'll lose all the families who have come from churches that baptize infants. And some of our members' husbands or wives are from these churches, yet they have joined here." Their dilemma prepared the way into the Bible and the Acts of the Apostles (10:47–48), and Calvin's words about Christians, infants, and baptism. That was 1959, in a parish that was struggling through practicing a sacrament with an openness that has not become an ecumenical discussion until now and the World Council of Churches' document *Baptism, Eucharist, and Ministry!* I look back to an official board and those hours of working out a compromise: infant baptism for families from that church tradition; adult baptism by pouring according to the congregation's heritage; with both performed as part of a service of worship and the second (as it always was) as part of the Service of Confirmation. The struggle to work out that compromise was another dimension of the word acceptability, a pastor being acceptable to the congregation and the congregation being acceptable to the pastor.

A church's "personality" may also be coded, written in furniture, memorial gifts, artwork, sacred to someone in the congregation. Enter pastor who rearranges the chancel chairs, and there is a crisis! Another moment to learn—after failing the exam. I flunked what could be called a quiz, which meant that I had an early warning. A seventh-generation member took me on a tour of the church, which had been constructed from trees and a quarry in the area. The building had its own story to tell through vaulting wooden arches, nearly twenty-foot-high paneled doors, and granite buttresses. Then the member asked what I thought of the three chairs behind the large, central pulpit. It was the time when fallout shelters were being debated. I answered, "They are almost large enough to serve as shelters!" She answered, "My father made them." I tried to turn my sarcasm into a compliment by adding, "They are very substantial, very substantial!" The woman had a sense of humor; she laughed as she watched me blush. I learned from that tour to listen and inquire and to withhold comment on objects and furnishings, knowing that there is a history recorded in them that remains hidden until a member proudly tells it.

"Knowing the congregation," its history, its theology, "read" in books, records, church activities, and conversations of members are sources for defining the word. Another source of information is a study of the pastors.

KNOWING THE PASTORS

Who served the congregation before your arrival? What kind of people were they?—not according to their pastoral records and biographies, if there are any, and if there are, look out! First, check the author. If it is the pastor, an autobiography, ponder the motivation for the tome. If it was written by a parishioner and that person or his or her family are still around, look out! There is a pedestal hiding somewhere and that pastor is still occupying it. If there is a portrait, you'd better bow regularly before it; if the church is a shrine to that pastor's ministry, then you'd better honor that pastor's memory, even if you did not know that pastor, or if you knew the person and were not impressed. Listening to parishioners extol that individual's "accomplishments" is a source of valuable information about the congregation's expectations for a pastor. In a congregation's praise and criticism of its previous pastors there are learnings, dos and don'ts for the new pastor. Another lesson taught by two parishes!

The current pastorate is a congregation established in 1854. I am its sixth pastor. The first served forty-two years; the fifth, thirty-two years; the second, six; the third and fourth, seventeen. There are no biographies, only brief church histories. The rest is waiting to be detected in parishioners' comments. I hear them talk about so-and-so's "fatherly ministry," and another's "scholarly, thought-provoking sermons," and still another "about which there isn't much to say except he was opposed to drinking and cards, and we hid both when he came to visit!" From those few comments a profile of the pastor can be written: a caring person who does not intimidate members, a person whose leadership helps us to be a church family, and a preacher whose sermons are meaningful; conversations of members defined their expectations for a pastor: preacher, counselor, visitor—their checklist for determining "acceptability."

On my second Sunday, Easter Sunday, at Trinity Church one elderly woman voiced her approval of my acceptability. With the recently retired pastor of thirty-two years standing on one side of her and I, the new pastor of one week, standing on the other side, she looked at the arrangement of flowers she made it her custom to place on the table in the church's lower vestibule. It was also her custom to give that Easter arrangement to the pastor. Looking at the retired pastor who had received her gift for all the years she placed it in the church, she announced, "These aren't for you. You ain't the pastor anymore. She is!" My predecessor graciously, quietly accepted her announcement, not as one of the hurtful realities of retirement, but as a signal of acceptance. She was letting a pastor's mantle pass from him to me. She was announcing in her "she is!" that this "she" is acceptable.

The first parish was a different story, not in the predecessors' years of service, but in the biography of the most recent pastor. Parishioners spoke of "his prayers; how close God felt when he prayed," and his sermons: "He took us into the pages of scripture; we felt we were there on Sinai, in Jerusalem, with Jesus." And then the conversation shifted to confusion or anger and the words, "That's why it was such a shock." The "it" meant "Don't push for more information. Let the rest of the story be told when a person is ready to finish it." In time the details were told: a brilliant seminarian who spent a year in the Holy Land before coming to the church to serve as assistant pastor, automatically named pastor five years later when the senior pastor's entire ministry spent on that congregation ended suddenly with his death at age sixty-nine, and then twenty-five years of service ending abruptly in an arrest, charges of sodomy, and a five-year prison sentence. A devastated congregation wavered between guilt, numbness, shock, and anger. Some demanded that action be taken to strip their former pastor of his ordination, but no one knew how to go about a defrocking, and none of the clergy wanted to learn the procedure.

My husband and I walked into that crisis, unaware of the emotions, unprepared to heal the wounds and work through the anger, but we accepted their call. That seemed to be the best action at that moment. By coming to them we were saying, "We accept you as well as your call." It was acceptance with a terrible cost—not to me, but to an imprisoned predecessor, and to my husband. After four or five years had passed I saw the lesson taught by that caring, scholarly pastor whose ministry was terminated by civil authorities and a twenty-five-year pastorate destroyed by gossip.

The lesson was: when a predecessor's ministry is a negative record by the pastor's and/or the congregation's assessment, the successor will be more readily accepted if there is little resemblance between the previous and the current minister. In the case of our predecessor in our first parish, my husband, being male, met with the warning, "We let the last pastor get away with 'murder'; we're going to make sure you don't get away with *anything!*" And he was watched. To relieve the tension we joked about their keeping a record even of the sheets of toilet paper he used! Being under surveillance certainly contributed to Howard's decision to practice his ministry as a full-time educator and a part-time supply pastor, plus being both Aaron and Hur to me.

At the same time, Howard and I remarked that I was free to "get away with 'murder.'" (I never explored what was meant by that word beyond its being a colloquialism.) I was watched too but in a different way. There was no model for a woman pastor; I was an unknown quantity, and so I was watched to see what I would do. When people saw me doing the things a pastor does, making calls, attending meetings, preparing sermons, they seemed pleased. I was directing my time to serving them. Somehow there were members who knew exactly how many hours I devoted to hospital and home visits and how long the lights were on in the study. Their verbal reports to one another were as accurate as my monthly statistical reports to the Diaconate! I took their scrutiny as an expression of interest, an "involvement" in my work as their pastor. But in their approval I also saw the price paid to accomplish that acceptance and another lesson learned by a clergywoman.

A WOMAN'S ADVANTAGE

Sometimes a clergywoman is at an advantage. She may be like a breath of fresh air, set a new direction, change a focus from anger and shame and defeat to hope and purpose— because she is a woman. She is not another man who may be like the last one "who failed us." This "advantage" is, of course, exercised at another's expense. Because my ministry began in that setting, I waited for a time when I could express my gratitude. It came in half-day visits with my predecessor when he was released from prison. Once a month he would have two days off from his job as a night clerk at a Salvation Army headquarters. He would spend this time visiting two families in the parish. One day I happened to walk into a home when he was there. No words were spoken until I reached out to shake his hand and say how much I welcomed a chance to visit. We became good friends, and he became my counselor, teacher of the congregation's particular Reformation heritage, source of sermon and devotional material, and my consultant when the congregation went into a quarter-million-dollar building program in the early 1960s. His blessing as well as his interest attended all my work. When a call came in 1972 from a coroner's office, announcing that his body had been found in his apartment, which had been stripped of all his art treasures and books, I felt an even heavier burden. I had been the recipient of his talents, and at his memorial service I felt the need to invite the few who attended to celebrate his gifts as I related the details no one knew to include in his biography. It was my feeble attempt to say thank you and to confess that my acceptance as a pastor was achieved by my failure and a church's failure to know how to minister to a man whose talents as a pastor were threatened by his needs—which no one dared to acknowledge. We still are struggling to see if we will ever learn, or be willing to accept, what is waiting to be taught to us by such people as my predecessor.

I would like to think that a clergywoman, accepted by a parish that needs a new focus, also learns to contribute a new perspective to the ministry: an appreciation for clergy, men and women, serving in less than positive situations. Pastors I once criticized as being ineffective, lazy, lacking in intelligence are clergy I now give a second look and a second opinion. The change has come because I look at the parish as well as the pastor and see that men as well as women may be serving congregations that provide inadequate salaries and no potential for satisfaction in the ministry. Clergywomen who "find a church to serve" because no male pastor would accept the call can also be advocates for men as well as women whose parishes are problem situations. A clergywoman's advantage may be her sensitivity to colleagues falsely judged because their ministry is being inaccurately appraised. But she sees, and she understands.

A WOMAN'S CHALLENGE

When a clergywoman is called to a parish that is not considered to be "a problem," the word acceptability becomes a challenge. Community, church, previous pastors provide the curriculum on the subject "how to behave in the parish"—a lesson that is a trap for a woman. Her acceptability depends on whether or not she accepts that lesson. It is not new. A seminary professor's last word to graduates going to their first parish has always been "Don't change anything the first year." That counsel is critical for a woman. Just by being a woman, a woman pastor brings newness, novelty, and curiosity to the church whose call she accepts. In my first years in the ministry I would be invited by a male pastor to come to speak with the explanation "They've never seen a woman minister." I would decline, sometimes with the excuse "I'm sorry, I don't have time to take my show on the road this week." Now I am serving a parish in which I often perform the service of marriage for previously divorced Roman Catholic couples. As the wedding processional begins and I take my place in the chancel, when I face the congregation, waiting for the bridal party to come down the aisle, it is not uncommon to watch Roman Catholic families look up, look again, and then whisper, "It's a woman!" Or "The 'sister' is a pastor!" That is the way it is! Just by being a woman, a woman pastor makes the pastoral ministry inclusive. There. I've said it! A statement that puts me in the middle of debate and controversy—especially with this illustration.

If a congregation has been accustomed to hearing their pastor begin a service of worship with the Trinitarian Ascription (Solemn Declaration), say it! At the *beginning* of your ministry, don't substitute a newer call to worship. Say, "In the name of the Father, and of the Son, and of the Holy Spirit." In saying those words a pastor who is a woman *is* filling them with new meaning simply because they are being said by a woman. A woman brings inclusiveness to the ministry by saying and doing what a congregation has heard and seen only a man say and do.

That I have been taught in the classroom of the parish is the *beginning* in the movement toward inclusive vocabulary and theology. To deny this lesson's validity is to jeopardize a woman's acceptability as pastor, implying that she does the parish ministry differently, which can be corrupted to a woman *should* do the ministry differently. I have attended clergywomen retreats dating back to the mid-1970s and listened to theologians analyze the pastoral ministry as a male-dominated office corrupted by a pastor-as-man image chiseled in stone. The only way to break that image is to break that stone into dust and start all over again with the office chiseled in the form of a woman who, in the words of one woman seminarian, "presents a different model."

I cannot accept that reasoning, and inclusive language is my reason. Inclusive language about God proves how inadequate human speech is, regardless of the language we choose. Our humanness shows when we involve ourselves in God-talk. We have no pronoun, we who are "he" or "she," for God, who is the perfect combination of both pronouns, is total completeness, while we, male and female, are always incomplete, only half of the Creator's wholeness. I make this application to the parish ministry. It is an office, a role, that because only men have filled it prompts some to hold to a pastor-as-man image, but that is only because they have not seen women in that office. My point is, it is not the office that needs to be changed, but the people who fill it—chapter 1's lesson, the need for women as well as men to be seen doing the work of a pastor. (This office and role and model of "pastor" has its own chapter, chapter 6.) In *this* chapter my learning and my urging is, because "she" isn't a man and only men are pastors, be a pastor according to the congregation's previous experience of the parish ministry, the denomination's standard, the denomination's historical-theological references to the work of a pastor; these are the essentials for a woman being accepted as pastor.

Change takes place in small steps. Once you have established trust, people will accept innovations more easily. In the matter of inclusive language, start with the spoken word and move on to the written word. It is better to use new material than to change the old, familiar words. *Fresh Winds of the Spirit, Whispers of God,* and *Refreshing Rains of the Living Word*—all written by Lavon Bayler—are worship resources based on the lectionary readings. Although they use inclusive language, their purpose is to enhance the flow of worship. *Bread for the Journey* and *Flames of the Spirit,* edited by Ruth Duck, have peace and justice themes. They can be used as resources for formal worship as well as for informal worship in various settings. Small-group study is a good opportunity to make people aware of women's concerns. An excellent book to facilitate this is *With Both Eyes Open: Seeing Beyond Gender,* edited by Patricia Altenbernd Johnson and Janet Kalven.

Another challenge for a woman is the very practical matter of being heard, which is labeled a "woman's problem." My observation is that the problem is shared by men;

in this age of elaborate communications systems that carry the human voice back and forth in space, worshipers may say to preachers, as one parishioner said to a young clergyman, "You chew your words!" Perhaps there is too much dependence on sound systems, assuming that someone will make the adjustments necessary to give volume and clarity to the voice. Or maybe there isn't enough attention given to being heard and being sensitive to the people who leave a church service or meeting saying, "I wish I could have heard what was said; I didn't get one word!"

I am indebted to two persons, Dr. Alfred N. Sayres, who said, "Preach to the back pew" and to my mother, who does not hesitate to announce, "My batteries are dead" (her hearing aid batteries!). That is my signal—and challenge—to make sure she can hear from her seat four rows beyond the pulpit. From my mother's monitoring my speech, indicating when words are audible and when they are being "chewed," I have learned three essentials to being heard. They are pitch, pause, pace.

Church members with hearing defects, especially tone deafness, report that they can hear an individual when the voice is pitched in the middle range, not high soprano, not rumbling bass. (Sorry, men, there is no discrimination when it comes to being heard; a male voice may be just as unsatisfactory as a female's, according to those straining to hear.) Speakers who are audible also pause at the end of a thought or phrase or sentence and pace their words so they are unhurried. There is time for the listener to follow what is being said. Pause and pace also make sermon preparation easier; less material is needed. I have noticed that the sermons I preach now are about half the volume of words counted in a sermon of twenty years ago, but the time remains the same. I've slowed down my pace, determined to be heard, for two reasons. One, to avoid learning my preparation was all in vain as someone announces when leaving, "I wish I could have heard what you said, but I couldn't hear a single word!" Two, to be supportive of my sisters in the ministry who will be dismissed as being inaudible for no other reason than their being a woman, with a woman's voice. I have also learned that some people, seeing a woman rise to speak, assume that she won't be heard, so they mentally turn off to her words.

This, too, is a personal experience. In the first parish several older people apologized that I could not be heard. I now know it was not my voice, but my gender. Only when guest male ministers stood in the same pulpit and preached words the same older people could not hear did their "hearing" improve, and they reported, "Someone must have worked on the P.A. system; now I can hear you."

At a recent clergy gathering, when I was invited to give the annual lecture on the subject of the parish ministry, I reviewed my paper for a reporter who wanted to write an article. When I mentioned the need for a pastor to be heard and how critical that is to a woman's being accepted as a pastor, *she* said, "I don't think that's too relevant a point. If you need to save time, I'd omit that reference." Irrelevant? Not by what worshipers report. Being heard is essential to being accepted. Pitch, pause, pace are essential to being an effective pastor; this lesson is a discipline imposed on men as well as women, with the difference being that a clergyman who cannot be heard may be tolerated, whereas a clergywoman is rejected. Another challenge for a woman.

Parishioners say what they feel about a pastor when the pastor is a woman, beginning with a woman's election as minister. The losing no votes often walk out, visibly, loudly, to a church close enough for everyone to note their departure long after they officially removed their membership to another congregation. That, too, has been a personal experience. In 1959 a family who joined the church during the time when it was being served by supply pastors left for another church a year after my election. When I visited them they politely explained that another church was closer to their home. When they talked with church members their reason was that they couldn't accept a woman minister. When our members reported that reason to me, they added, "It's really because they know we're going into a building program; they want to get out before they are asked to give." I wonder what has happened to that family; the church they joined has had its own building program and costly pipe organ renovation, and is now served by a woman pastor.

In the current parish a woman, against the pleas of her closest friends to "give her a chance; you'll really come to like her," transferred her membership to another church of our denomination less than a mile away. With that transfer a question began to be raised: "Was I the reason or the convenient excuse?" Friends have questioned why she had ever joined the church from which she was transferring; her background and theological orientation were not at all compatible with the congregation's worship and doctrine. How much of that incompatibility was hidden under the statement "I can't accept a woman minister!"? That question teaches me a lesson I find difficult to learn and even harder to accept: parishioners don't stifle feelings and opinions when the pastor is a woman, and they may use the woman as a cover, a dodge, a convenient excuse for leaving the congregation. That learning creates a dilemma for me: probe or let it pass? When the excuse maker (making me the subject of her excuse for leaving the church) moves on to another church, I have let that person's excuse pass, exploring it only with those who stay. My practice has usually proved to be the correct choice—another lesson—

because those who stay sometimes feel embarrassed, even hurt, by their friend's words and actions. It is a rejection of their counsel and, more than that, of their friendship, and in their attempt to work through the person's decision they often reveal other reasons. I was the "cover" for dissatisfactions that were brewing and heating up over a period of time, long before my time. A learning that has prompted me to turn to satire and ask, "Do you want difficult church members to have a way out? Call a woman to be your pastor; then they can use her coming as their excuse for leaving, rather than having to admit that the real reason is they are the problem!" That is a point to add to a manual on effective pastoral leadership if a clergywoman's call to a church rids the congregation of some of its less-than-supportive members.

Leadership is another challenge, especially for a woman who has not had an introduction to such books as Claude Steiner's *The Other Side of Power;* Hilary M. Lips' *Women, Men, and the Psychology of Power;* Nancy M. Henley's *Body Politics: Power, Sex, and Non-verbal Communication.* In the classroom of the parish the first lesson was to learn my predecessor's style of leadership and how that style was perceived, which was a learning in itself. The lesson was a congregation's perception of a pastor's leadership and that pastor's self-perception. A pastor who is comfortable with his or her faults and strengths, not afraid to lead, and open to suggestions, honoring a member's talents and using them; a person who can be a leader and a team member, practicing the office of pastor as a shared ministry (to which chapter 6 is devoted), is a pastor who is involved in learning and practicing "leadership." But when a woman takes on the office of pastor, she may need to answer some questions before assuming the leadership of a congregation, such questions as, How well have I prepared myself to lead? How comfortable am I under pressure, in decision-making, in managing and supervising? Am I straightforward, or indirect, devious? How have I been "programmed" by my parents, teachers, friends to lead, or not to lead? What is my perception of myself as a leader? In one short question: How do I go about leading?

There are courses. One or more may be worth every minute and dollar given to that pursuit. There are magazines written for business executives and corporate officers; a subscription may be a wise expenditure. And a related subject, Assertiveness Training, is another exploration. A professor gave me a six-page quiz on "How do you react when . . ."-type questions. I did not get past the first page before I realized that I was accumulating a much higher score than the accepted norm. Reason: I am a pastor. My built-in reaction is "Don't antagonize. Be polite, apologetic, nonaggressive. Maintain 'ministerial manners.'" (Translated: "Don't let yourself act human.") I am continually caught in an inner debate of when to be verbally aggressive and when to remain silent. That is an intense dilemma for a leader who is a pastor, which has an added dimension for a woman. A question for a clergywoman: "Are you, when vocal and assertive, labeled 'pushy,' or 'nagging,' or 'hot-headed,' or a you-know-what-offspring-of-a-dog?" Self-perception and others' perception are two observations I consider critical to a woman's ministry and her role as leader. They probably rank above any training to perform pastoral functions, for the way a woman is perceived as a leader is the real test of her effectiveness as a pastor. For a woman, it can be a Catch-22 but there is a way out.

Again, I return to the homework of knowing your predecessors. What was the leadership style of previous pastors? Not their training, but their conduct as perceived and reported by the congregation. What style received high praise, which pastor is not mentioned, or named with a reserve and coolness that tells you "Let that one pass"? Adopt the leadership style that was appreciated, knowing that that model encourages a new pastor's acceptance; then "after the first year" move toward the leadership style that is appropriate, comfortable, natural.

There are resources for that movement: a denomination's and a congregation's constitution and bylaws. A woman who came from seminary to a pastorate, placed in a small church by a bishop, soon learned that there was no previous leadership model to adopt, if only for the first year. Predecessors were a parade of unique personalities. One was a retired minister who lived miles away and came only for Sunday services. Another was so casual in his leadership style that nothing was planned; worship was "Let's sing hymn number . . ." with the service following the whim of the pastor, not the liturgy of the denomination. Still another, her immediate predecessor, was so "high church" that the congregation jumped from an evangelical, free church tradition to Anglo-Catholic in a year's time. First meeting, first item on the agenda, the new pastor introduced the members of the committee to their denomination's manual on church organization and job descriptions for clergy and laity. She moved the focus of leadership from the hodgepodge history they had experienced and the questions they had when she arrived to an impersonal reference both could study and adopt. That seminary graduate who was twenty-five years younger than I was, with only one month's experience in the ministry, became my teacher! There is, however, another lesson in the curriculum of "acceptability" that lacks an instructor. It is a Catch-22 that, as yet, has no way out.

A WOMAN'S DILEMMA

The Catch-22 is the woman for whom a woman pastor is a disturbing presence. In chapter 3 I called this a reality that expands sexual harassment from a clergywoman to a congregation in which a woman pastor will meet victims of that harassment who will, in turn, victimize their new pastor. My first experience was total frustration, which I did not know how to handle until I looked past the women who were continually criticizing my actions to the families in which they lived. Such households were an American scene of the old German words: *Küche, Kinder, Kirche* (kitchen, children, church)—a woman's work and a woman's place. The women spent the entire morning in the kitchen preparing the full-course noonday meal. The men gathered around a large table that almost filled a spacious room. After they had been served, the women were permitted to take their places at the table. When I visited one of these households for the first time, the patriarch of the family, seated at the head of the table, announced, "Martha, sit down!" I sat with the men who were waiting for their meal, and I watched the women hurrying around the kitchen. It was a Catch-22. If I had refused to sit with the men, I would have denied "the patriarch's" acknowledgment of my being the new pastor, whom he was welcoming to his home and table. By sitting with the men, however, I alienated myself from my gender—assigned to the kitchen, and the bedroom. In that household women served two purposes: to satisfy the male hunger for food and for sex. For those women there was no freedom to pursue an education, nor was there money available to them to break away and choose a new life-style. Their home was their prison;

when I visited them I realized that I was visiting prisoners! And more. I was a reminder of what they were not free to be. Their protest took a form I needed a decade to learn to understand.

They complained loudly when I did not visit them enough; when I did visit they remained silent. Our conversations were monologues, which they later made the material for more criticism. Two women came to church only when I was on vacation; their reason, "We can't hear her." No one else experienced that difficulty. It was obvious that their "deafness" was rejection of the new pastor. At first I tried to encourage them, to compliment them: "You make perfect pie crusts; I'll never be able to match them! Your cross-stitch is beautiful!" My words were sincere—and ineffective! My compliments only served to remind them of work that imprisoned them in a household in which only the men were free to get away from the homestead. "How can I reach them?" I asked a church member who was their friend and neighbor. "Don't," she counseled. "Go to them when they need a pastor; stay away when they don't need you." Another teacher, another lesson! They could not accept me as a woman, but they did accept me as a pastor. They separated who I was (a woman enjoying a freedom they did not have) from what I did. I had to accept being a split personality in their company, to be acceptable to them as their pastor. It was an uncomfortable adaptation and a painful lesson that took me back to the last line of the early Christians' "Hymn of Love" (1 Corinthians 13:13): "So faith, hope, love abide, these three; but the greatest of these is love." "Love," that was the word I had to learn to make the gauge of my relationship with women whose lives were walled in by the words *Küche, Kinder, Kirche*. It was also the word I learned to make *the* word for ministry, a word that deserves its own chapter.

5 • CHARITY

The Classroom

When I was a member of our regional denominational staff I visited many pastors and churches. One of the most pleasant visits was to a parsonage and three congregations in the far corner of the region.

During a Sunday dinner with the pastor I inquired about the previous pastors. The names recalled tension-filled years, unhappy pastors and unhappy parishioners, both ready to engage in verbal combat that ended only when the pastor resigned. A new pastor signaled a new round of ecclesiastical warfare, until the current pastor arrived, and the peace became more than a stalemate or a truce. I had to know what brought about the change, which is so obvious.

The pastor's answer: "When I came here I was told how difficult the people were and how short my stay would probably be. I decided the minute I came that I would love them into life. And that's what I have done all these years. I just love them!"

The pastor's decision is proof of the wisdom of his choice; he has stayed longer than any predecessor and hesitates to leave even though he could have retired several years ago. His answer is a lesson that I intended to include in the previous chapter—until I gave his answer some thought. Love: the motivation for ministry that qualifies visibility, identity, realities, and acceptability. Love is a curriculum in itself.

The Lesson

When a woman is seen as a person who loves being a pastor, that visibility and identity encourage acceptance and temper realities. Love engenders love, but not without learning its dimensions in the parish ministry.

LOVING ONE'S SELF

Self love. The capacity to love one's self, celebrating strengths, accepting weaknesses, confessing peculiarities. My personal model teacher was Bela Vassady, whose tongue was shaved during his internment as a World War II prisoner of the Nazis, causing him to lisp. He also speaks English with a Hungarian accent, revealing his native country. When Dr. Vassady came to Lancaster Theological Seminary in Pennsylvania, his annual delight was to welcome students to his home and invite them to impersonate him, especially his lisp. He roared with laughter as each of us tried to copy his speech impediment! In the Vassady living room I was introduced to learning to accept my peculiarities: my bird's-eye vision, having only one "good" eye—a readily observed handicap. Dr. Vassady taught me to be the first to laugh at myself and to accept what I cannot change. He taught me to love the person I am.

Living with scars, not open wounds. The hard work of working through personal problems such as divorce, or sexual orientation, or harassment is best done before accepting a call to ministry, so that the pastorate is not a platform for protesting unresolved personal hurts or angers, but the ministry of a person who is sensitive to others' pain because he or she has known pain.

Accepting personal limitations. A woman may find this expression of self-love to be an impossibility; I did—a confession made in the past tense for two reasons. One reason I implied in an earlier chapter; I realized that I would not survive if I kept going at the pace I kept in my first years in the ministry. The second, I accepted the counsel of a retired pastor: "The more you do, the more they'll expect!" which would have led to burning out sooner and turning from love to hate. I would have hated the people I was lovingly serving. But it was not easy to confess my limitations. It was a risk I at first determined would threaten my acceptance. I needed to learn from my younger sisters in the ministry, who chided me for not celebrating my assets, which I had to learn is part of accepting my limitations. I had to learn to name my strengths, gratefully (not arrogantly), as another dimension of love, loving the person I am. That is still an uncomfortable exercise for me, but I do it for my sisters in the ministry; celebrating who I am is also honoring who they are. And the limitations follow. They are an admission to my being human, not feminine, an admission that grows in length when I look beyond self to family.

Remembering the family. A pastor's common confession

is that life is a tug-of-war between guilt over time spent in the parish and time spent with the family. Love means learning to say no to writing in all the spaces in the calendar; to leaving no open time for spouse, children, self, recreation, entertainment, or doing nothing; and to blocking out distractions. I do not do this well! Right now, as I am writing, an aroma is filling the air that signals the supper is burning. It's the rice. I became so involved in putting thoughts into words that I forgot to turn the heat under the rice from "High" to "Simmer!" The dogs will have their food supplemented with burned rice. This time there is enough rice to cook more servings, which I will watch and let the writing wait. Proof that I am far from being a scholar in this dimension of love!

Loving the unlovable self. There is another aspect to "loving one's self" that is unlovable: the absence of admirable traits and talents, deficiencies in ability or in training, a subject I want to avoid but cannot because of love.

Elouise Renich Fraser, assistant professor of systematic theology at Eastern Baptist Theological Seminary, near Philadelphia, raised this issue when she addressed the 1986 Evangelical Round Table held at Eastern College, St. Davids, Pennsylvania. Her comment was "lower expectations for women and minorities. This is an increasingly troublesome pattern in theological education. The problem is this: women and minorities are sometimes allowed to pass through programs without being confronted regarding their inability to perform at acceptable levels." Dr. Fraser's word for this pattern is "inhumanity" and the "refusal to enter into the struggle of relationship with them." Anything less is a prompting to "cynicism and contempt." How does a person love self and others when he or she discovers and admits that he or she has become a victim of a system that did not prepare him or her for ministry?

That question may seem out of place in this chapter. Logic would place it in chapter 1, addressing it to denominational and judicatory executives, committees charged with the care of seminarians, and the seminarians themselves. Because few are assuming that responsibility and risk—the risk of questioning a woman's personal qualifications for ministry—I place the question in this chapter, with the victim who, when trying to love one's self, realizes that there are some unlovely details. As long as those contributing to the "troublesome pattern" do nothing about it, the person whose preparation for ministry is deficient must be the one who faces the fact of feeling cheated and turning cynical or becoming contemptuous. I protest the systems that are responsible for those reactions. I feel the pain of individuals who must decide whether or not their lack of preparation for ministry renders them unsuitable for ministry, a decision forced on them because others did not dare to counsel as an expression of love.

LOVING THE CONGREGATION

Forgetting labels. "What's your sign?" is an early question raised in conversations, a label, making a person's biography the lines in a horoscope. There is also blood type, metabolism, cardiac history—more labels. Astronomy, hematology, physiology, psychology—classifications that love teaches a pastor to ignore. Love's invitation is to turn a person's life into a treasure hunt to find all that is lovable in that person's life. It is a search to discover what lies beyond, behind, beneath the unlovely details. It is a search for the likeness of God. Where is it? How is God's image represented in this person's life? Years ago a parishioner gave me the words to say in silence when meeting someone new: "The Christ in me greets the Christ in you!" Then she added, "The greater the distance between the two of you, a distance marked by anger or hatred or prejudice, the more you say the words, 'The Christ in me . . . in you!'" Her counsel directs my search to find the evidence of love in another's life. It is a discovery made through listening to another's life story. And in listening, even the unlovely may bond listener to storyteller. That, to me, is a pastor's privilege, to have the time and to use time listening to a parishioner's life story; it is the privilege of being invited to be part of that person's life. That alone is a reason to feel love for that person. It is the love of being trusted not to turn what has been shared into next Sunday's sermon illustration, or the next case study for a course in pastoral counseling. My joy is to sit in someone's home, or ride with members to a meeting or funeral, and share stories, theirs and mine. And then to hear a confession spoken in response to trust. That is love which nurtures love!

I am learning to give this dimension of love new expressions. As medical service becomes more complex and a hospital stay is limited to intensive or critical care, I find myself becoming a pastoral advocate, working with the parishioner-patient to determine what questions about his or her care need answers, tactfully inquiring of medical staff, indicating the patient's anxieties. Then there is the patient's family with their needs: to know what questions to ask, to understand the alternatives for posthospital care, to select the option that is best for the patient and his or her family. One Friday I walked into a hospital room to visit with an elderly church member; it was also an entrance into a crisis. The patient and her sister were protesting a social worker's announcement that the patient was going to be sent home. "Everything is going to be fine. All your needs will be taken care of! A visiting nurse will stop and you'll have Meals on Wheels." I wondered how! The patient's heart condition confined her to a bed; she lived alone; her sister was too ill to care for her; neighbors were not available; and the area's Meals on Wheels program had a waiting list. In the course of being too direct in the past, I learned not to challenge the social worker's announced plan. I was oblique. "Oh, that's wonderful that meals will be available. Several others in our area have had to wait." The social worker asked, "Where does the patient live?" Her sister answered, "Collegeville." The social worker left the room. Her first stop must have been to check the Collegeville area and to discover the length of the waiting list. The patient was not sent home, but to a nursing home. Just what the patient and her sister had wanted but were earlier denied. The crisis was averted through my newly learned exercise of love.

There is another dimension to a pastor's love for her or his congregation that is so new the details are not known; the classroom and its lesson can only be anticipated. It is the pastor's changing role as prearranged funerals become a new venture for investors and nationwide funeral homes. How will a pastor serve a parishioner at the time of the death of a spouse when that couple "signed up" years ago for a "package" that included everything, including the corporation's chapel, bereavement counselor, and chaplain? I find myself needing to learn how to serve when I'll be a person perceived as not needed by a funeral home's "fully professional staff," and I'll need to learn how to handle resentment, which is the last thing a grieving member needs from the pastor! How to love when denied by others whom I may perceive are serving unlovingly is one of life's exams I do not welcome taking. But I'll take it if it is scheduled sometime in the future—because of love.

Continuing education is the name for new lessons needing to be learned, and love prompts participation. To stagnate spiritually and mentally is to impose that stagnation on an entire congregation. To continue to learn is to share what is learned, to give parishioners the same opportunity, to be students together. In that mutual sharing there is a mutual experience of love.

There are also the older, established "courses" on loving a congregation, such as learning to acknowledge reality. Love means determining what can be changed and what cannot; distinguishing essentials from nonessentials; deciding which issues are critical and which are not. Love means asking, "How much better will the congregation and community be because of priorities I set as the agenda for my ministry?" Or "Are my decisions imposed on others because I don't trust them? Am I a dictator, or a pastor who shares decision-making with the people I serve?" Another expression of trust and love.

Reality also means accepting disagreement, letting people express themselves and their opinions—controversial, contradictory, volatile opinions. When they do they test my capacity to love, and I regularly prove that I have much more to learn. I get too involved in the noise of a person's words and fail to realize that permitting an individual to "ventilate" is an exercise of love. This lesson, however, has another dimension, an antithesis, which makes its exam difficult to pass, at least for me. The tough question is when and how to deal with a member whose outbursts are a threat to the congregation's peace or another member's dignity and rights. Love calls for accountability and sensitivity. How to speak truth in love is a testing that forces me to spend hours practicing what words to say and anticipating what response my words might elicit. I am learning that the word truth is a good teacher. To be truthful in voicing my concerns for the well-being of the congregation and my love for the person whose words or actions are perceived as being empty of love. This test is given to me regularly, and each time I am showing a slight improvement in my score as I learn that the results depend on my willingness to be truthful.

When a family with young children, ages two through eight, appeared one Sunday morning, they were immediately welcomed, taken on a tour of the church facilities, introduced to everyone along the way, and given the standard literature about the congregation. The next Sunday they came the welcome was repeated along with their names. They were a real "find"—an interested couple; children for the church school, cherub choir, and junior choir; and a husband and wife for the newly formed young adult class. They, too, were impressed. And then they told their story. They were church shopping, and they had a shopping list. This would be their second church since their marriage. They had decided to leave the congregation where they were baptized, confirmed, married. They no longer agreed with what was being preached. In their shopping they had found a church that matched their list, but it was too far from their home. Our church sign carried the same denominational name, but the sign is the only similarity. The other church has drawn up its own statement of faith, which all members must affirm; its theological stance is closer to neighboring independent-fundamentalist churches; and it regularly engages in "sheep stealing," even to the near-death of churches of the same denomination.

The father, exercising his authority, asked whether or not we used the statement of the "true" church he had found for his family. His question revealed his intention to join a church like the one he had located, or to make it his mission to help this church be like that church. Rather than stealing sheep, he would save us and then join us. I suggested that he continue to search, naming an independent church close to his home. That, too, is love's lesson, not to let the desire for more members welcome some who will be unwelcome, by their own and the congregation's judgment. Truth's lesson: to admit that those who are church shopping must be pointed toward a church that matches their description. That is another exercise of love I am slowly learning.

Accepting the unacceptable, the unchangeable, the disruptive and difficult who are in the congregation is another lesson that I can now say it is possible to learn. My teacher was a "personality" in the fullest sense of the word, a well-educated, proper woman whose most recent goal was to outlive her grandmother, who died at the age of ninety-nine years, four months. She did; she lived 100 years, two months. That spunk carried her through personal tragedies that would have paralyzed others, emotionally and spiritually, but she feminized the role of Job and at the same time played the part of a Victorian lady. But in her last years, when I met her, her fortitude turned into an independence expressed in precise, sharp words. The faithful wife of the congregation's retired pastor visited the woman every Thursday, knowing the once-proud lady was now very lonely, a loneliness imposed by her harsh words; her insults drove away those who had been her friends. The one faithful person not only visited but came with gifts. Delicious homemade chocolate, the woman's favorite food, and freshly cooked vegetable soup, of which was said, "After I added some salt and sugar, I was able to eat it!" It was a typical response over which the woman's daughter, the bearer of gifts, and I laughed. And in laughing we learned.

The lesson: not to take an insulting person too seriously, to accept her words as her uniqueness. In time I came to enjoy visiting in her home. I visited with a goal: to see how she would insult me and to be disappointed if a visit passed without at least one insult. I may have read too much into later visits, but they seemed to be marked with fewer and fewer insulting comments, or was I learning how to let humor defuse them? There is an emptiness in my calling schedule now. I miss those afternoons when I was a student sitting in that woman's living room, learning how to love those considered to be less than lovable.

LOVING THE MINISTRY

In learning how to love a congregation, a pastor also learns how to love being a pastor. For me the lesson is learned by learning to practice one word: discipline. A word toward which I have worked my way by means of confession, the confession of how undisciplined my schedule was. A typical week in my practice of ministry looked organized: in the parsonage in the mornings, calls in the afternoons, meetings at night, a schedule altered only by emergencies. But it was a disordered order. I was in the parsonage study in the mornings—in my pajamas. I'd get involved in reading or phone calls and not take time to get dressed. And so while still in my pajamas I entertained the butcher, the milkman, the sexton, Mormons, and Jehovah's Witnesses, which prompted the church secretary to remark, "You get more wear out of your clothes than anyone else around here!" "How can that be?" I asked. "Because you spend so much of the day in your pajamas!" It was not enough of an urging to get me to change my morning routine. I went on from embarrassment to embarrassment in my first years in the ministry.

And then there was my sermon preparation routine. I'd work at least a month ahead, with files of references and notes: scripture, title, brief outline. But I wouldn't sit down to put all the pieces of paper into a sermon until 9:00 P.M. Saturday night, after the children were in bed, and Howard would pursue his hobby of classic car restoration in the garage. By 2:00 A.M. I would add the "Amen" to the sermon manuscript and then get up at 6:00 A.M. to go over the service, prayers, sermon, stopping at 8:30 to get dressed and run (literally) across the lawn to church and the church school class I taught at 9:00 A.M. It was a schedule, but a schedule that lacked discipline—which I learned when moving to the current parish—was an absence of love for the ministry. I did not like the Saturday night tension, nor could I enjoy Sunday afternoons. I was too mentally and physically exhausted, but not exhausted enough to say, "This is ridiculous!" The call to serve on the Conference staff broke that pattern, and the call to the current pastorate was a new start, a new test of my response to the word discipline. From the first week on I let that word teach me how to love being in the ministry. The lesson began with getting up and getting dressed, a discipline necessitated by spending the morning in the pastor's study at church, not at home. That slight change taught an unexpected lesson, another dimension of love. By being at church each weekday morning, making calls in the afternoon, attending meetings, and counseling sessions at night—a pattern with exceptions, but not too many—that routine makes my week fairly predictable. And that is the lesson: in routine there is security and security nurtures a bond of love between pastor and congregation—and community. To know when I am accessible is to feel that I am available, and both are a mutual expression of love. It is a lesson I am enjoying and it began when I adopted a morning discipline that spares me entertaining the public in my pajamas!

There is an exception to the weekly schedule: Tuesday, the day that enhances my love for the ministry, because it is the new discipline that replaces the old, ridiculous routine for preparing a sermon. No more weekly five-hour marathons followed by four hours' sleep! Now it is Tuesday. All day and night Tuesday, except for emergencies or a once-a-month evening meeting. I love Tuesdays. They are the day I spend finishing the next Sunday's order of worship, reading, meditating, preparing the sermon. And when the sermon doesn't take shape, I lay it aside—until Friday if necessary, and when necessary the sermon is finished on Friday. There is time to change the outline or even the direction, to add, to delete, to live the message, testing it against the background of a week. Tuesday is my very special day, a retreat, from which I emerge refreshed, renewed, ready to spend the rest of the week in the parish and the world. Tuesday is my day to fall in love all over again with the work of being a pastor. Tuesday is a discipline the congregation helps me to keep. If on a Tuesday I am seen in town or at church, I am made to answer, "What are you doing out today? This is Tuesday. You should be home!" A pause usually follows and then, "What kind of sermon are we going to get on Sunday?" The second question implies the sermon won't be a good one because I'm "out" on Tuesday. In response I clear myself with one of three excuses: "The choir has the sermon; they're giving a cantata." Or "We have a guest speaker." Or "I'll be on vacation." That ritual of questions and answers is another reminder of our bond of love.

And then there is Saturday, sometime, whatever time is available, when I take an hour or two to go over the sermon and the service and my other details for Sunday. Saturday, too, has its special moment, when I review the week in prayer. What has happened in the world, the community, the parish? Who has reasons to rejoice, to confess, to weep, to feel anxious, angry, rebellious? Saturday's special moment is that time when, in the tradition of the early church's bidding prayers, I ponder Sunday morning's prayer-conversation with God at the altar table. What are the words for our church family's offering of prayer? How I cherish that Saturday hour! It is my personal moment to review another week of work and why I love being a pastor.

Love! The word that qualifies, defines, and enhances the ministry, and prompts another lesson: a definition of the word ministry. What are the specifics of this work that nurtures love in the dimensions described in this chapter? And so one more chapter, a chapter devoted to "ministry."

6 • MINISTRY

The Classroom

It wasn't a standing room audience and the discussion was a polite conversation, not the polarized debate anticipated by the subject of women's ordination. Those who were opposed stayed away; only those in favor came to "Open Dialogue," a regular after-lunch event at Ursinus College. Real dialogue had to wait until after the scheduled debate was closed with a thank you to the participants. After circulating around the college's lounge, I began to talk with a student who, during the discussion, had identified herself as being for women's rights in the church as well as in the world of business. Her stand was motivated by her reaction to her education in a Roman Catholic parochial school system, where she acquired the impression that clergy are "too bossy."

My response to her impression was "That is not my understanding or my practice of ministry. I see myself as a 'servant'—'a servant of the servants of God.'" The student looked puzzled. "Servant," she said, "I've never heard anything like that said before." She wanted to think about what she identified as "an intriguing definition."

In her response I found myself being taught by my own answer!

The Lesson

A pastor is a servant. But what is the pastor's servant role? What is the office of pastor? Questions with differing answers or answers that are being challenged, especially by women. A student who was attending a seminary where women in the parish ministry are referred to as "pastors who happen to be women" voiced her resentment to those words, which I, too, have used to refer to myself. I am a pastor who happens to be a woman. In saying that, I am making a statement about the office of pastor. I believe that it is an office with specific functions, a role that can be defined and must be, for the well-being of women serving as pastors. Without definition, without a "norm," there is no reference for evaluation, no standard from which to deviate when deviations are appropriate, and no basis for assessing a clergyperson's ministry, a threat to men and women. Defining the office of pastor is, for me, the first assignment in this chapter's lesson.

THE OFFICE OF PASTOR

Of course there are the New Testament rules often intoned at the time of ordination: "to preach the message, to insist upon proclaiming it (whether the time is right or not), to convince, reproach, and encourage, as you teach with all patience [2 Tim. 4:2, TEV]." A verse that provides two defining verbs: preach and teach. And there is 1 Peter 5:1–2, TEV: "I appeal to you to be shepherds of the flock that God gave you and to take care of it willingly." Counsel that goes on to define "shepherds" as examples of caring service, words that provide a definition for "pastor," another form of the word shepherd.

Preach, teach, shepherd—the New Testament's description of elder or presbyter as it began to take on form and function in the early church. And now that definition is an open invitation to ecumenical dialogue as the World Council of Church's *Baptism, Eucharist, and Ministry* returns to the use of the terms bishops, presbyters, deacons, and defines the pastoral office as follows:

Presbyters serve as pastoral ministers of Word and sacraments in a local eucharistic community. They are preachers and teachers of the faith, exercise pastoral care, and bear responsibility for the discipline of the congregation to the end that the world may believe and that the entire membership of the Church may be renewed, strengthened and equipped in ministry. Presbyters have particular responsibility for the preparation of members for Christian life and ministry.　　　　　(*Ministry*. III C.30)

This definition, as I read it, prompts me to wonder, "What is the perceived definition? the perception acquired from clergy mentors, seminary courses in practical theology, and a congregation's expectations and impressions?" In the early 1970s a researcher interviewed me. She observed that pastors in the United Church of Christ tended to be individuals whose occupational interests grouped them with educators beyond the high school level. She added that pastors in more fundamentalist churches, when evaluated through the same vocational testing, ranked as "actors" or "salespersons." I think that little-publicized finding is revealing. It made the distinction, in the early 1970s, between pastors functioning as educators and others whose style was more flamboyant, actors in the pulpit, high-pressure salespersons in the street. Women must struggle through these characterizations of the pastoral ministry, seeing them not only as a question of the style that is most typical of a pastor's servant role, but also as perceptions with some old, unwelcome images, such as Aimee McPherson and a few more recent "evangelists." The educator image, however, leaves an unanswered question: "Education to do what?"

In the January 1978 issue of *Andover Newton Quarterly*, Ernest E. Klein wrote a tribute to Samuel H. Miller. The publication would not have come to my attention if it had not been given to me by a clergyperson who is one of my mentors. I realized that there was a double intention; it was given not only as a suggested norm for my ministry, a definition of what I had been educated to do, but as a hoped-for commentary on the ministry of the pastor who had saved the article. It was a statement of a norm my mentor wanted to emulate. Preacher, teacher-theologian, artist and poet, and a private person (meaning a person in touch with loneliness, suffering, and life's moments to celebrate), words describing what could be called the "traditional" style of the parish ministry.

In a 1986 issue of a bulletin from Philadelphia's Lutheran Seminary a black woman with eighteen months' experience as the pastor of a Lutheran congregation in Jersey City, New Jersey described her ministry as preaching, teaching, visiting, working to develop lay leadership in the congregation—and to have personal time to play the guitar, read, reflect, meditate, grow, and take some courses, not for a degree, but to broaden and enhance her talents. Without knowing Gladys Geraldine Moore, I admire her as she introduces herself through those words. Hers is also a "traditional" definition of the parish ministry.

In *The Clergy Journal,* February 1985, G. Lloyd Rediger attempted a different definition through questions: "What are my reference points for ministry? Am I engaged in discovering who I am? Am I open to God? Am I in touch with people? Do I trust my decision-making? Am I continuing to grow mentally, spiritually? Am I developing my skills to make them better; am I developing the skills of others?" Rediger shifted the definition from preaching, teaching, shepherding to "excellence" defined as "faithfulness." His focus is a shift I'd like to praise later in this chapter, but it is not a perceived emphasis. When asked to define a pastor's role, a congregation's answer is not a reply to Rediger's questions, but to the "preaching, teaching, shepherding" definition, which is what I heard when I asked.

The occasion was a conversation with a women's group in the church. During their meeting I conducted an informal survey, asking each person to list the responsibilities of a pastor, naming them in descending order of importance. Their response was the "traditional" definition and order. First, sermons and conducting worship, then teaching, and finally visiting, counseling, and such pastoral functions as weddings, baptisms, and funerals. Administration; meetings of the congregation, Association, Conference community; and involvement in human service agencies were not mentioned. When I listed a pastor's typical involvements in the order of hours spent doing each facet of the ministry, the work they had not mentioned appeared on the list and accounted for time needed for sermon preparation and visitation, a discrepancy that shifted my priorities in my first parish so that time spent in meetings and administration absorbed hours I wanted to spend studying and visiting. Now I intentionally reorder my priorities to put sermon preparation first, followed by visitation, counseling, meetings, and administration. The same answer the women's group gave when they responded to my invitation to define a pastor's work; my current "norm" as a pastor-servant, because my place of service, my first responsibility, is the congregation. This doesn't mean that I refuse to serve my Conference, denomination, community, and ecumenical endeavors. I am involved in all those areas, but that involvement must not distract from my first responsibility, the congregation, a statement that requires further definition.

I do not consider myself indispensable in the parish, nor do I function in the old role of "Herr Pastor," in charge, in command of everything. That is not my style or motivation. Responsibilities are shared; ours is a mutual ministry at Trinity Church (more on that subject in the next section). I am involved in the services, organizations, programs—if only to be visible—so that I may be found when a pastor's services are needed. And I am around, available, visible for another reason—to keep in touch with the congregation; to know their joys and sorrows; to be sensitive, alert, in tune; to be present in the life of the church so that the people I serve can give direction to my sermons, prayers, and studies. If I distance myself from the congregation by miles or by distracting activities, I will cut the lifeline that sustains my ministry. I need each member of Trinity Church more than any one of them needs me. They are the leaven in my service, my reason for being their pastor-servant.

As I reflect, I see my definition of the office of pastor is not a choice between the traditional words: preaching, teaching, shepherding and G. Lloyd Rediger's questions of excellence and faithfulness. In desiring to be faithful I have come to claim as "norm" that which is "traditional."

A PASTOR'S INITIATIVE

I must pursue the word teaching. It is taking on a new dimension. Our congregation is experiencing the joy of welcoming new members. They come from many, varying religious experiences and denominational backgrounds—a growing trend across our nation, studied by Lyle Schaller and Douglas Walrath, documented by Gallup polls, and illustrated in this story.

In the past year Trinity Church has welcomed enough young couples to form a new church school class. They are like fresh air, filled with energy, ideas, and a mix of theology that prompts some interesting questions. On Sunday mornings they teach themselves, another joy that relieves the Christian education committee of the wearisome chore of finding a teacher. The discussions are, however, emitting signals, signs of trouble that could be brewing, the "trouble" that comes when adults are not offered sound doctrine, a background in church history, and worship as well as the Bible. I "read" the signals as a sign that I must heed, a responsibility I as pastor must assume, for the pastoral office includes "teaching." I must take the initiative in providing Bible study resources, and I must teach some courses that will enable young adults to make up for deficiencies in their Christian education, a failing that is not theirs but mine. I am part of a generation or more of church activities that lacked substance and contributed to an increasing rate of spiritual illiteracy. But even in this initiative my intention is to initiate, to teach a few who, in turn, will teach, for I am not only a pastor-servant; I am also a servant of the servants of God, the laity. Another "office" needing definition.

THE OFFICE OF LAITY

After I read a paper at a theological symposium, a laywoman introduced herself by offering to buy me a soda. I should have accepted. Sipping from a can or through a straw would have been a pleasant diversion as I stood and listened to years of a layperson's anger at clergy compressed into an hour. It did not matter that I was a clergywoman; my description of our "mutual" ministry at Trinity Church was also unacceptable. Stories of laypeople planning Sunday services with me; of a committee of three who monthly create an every-Sunday "Children-in-Church" page and in the course of putting together that folder inspire sermon thoughts beyond my sensitivity or perception; examples of a Christian education committee generating experiences in ministry for children and adults involved in One-Great-Hour-of-Sharing, food for an inner-city mission, school kits for Church World Service; illustrations of Frank Laubach's "Each one teach one" adapted to "Each one recruit one" for service in the congregation, community, and Conference—all these meant nothing. The laywoman was unimpressed by a congregation whose members serve as volunteers in their municipalities and in more than twenty organizations, nor did she yield in her protest when I told of individuals whose Christian faith prompts their actions on the job, like the person who could retire and looks forward to retirement when she will devote much of her time to volunteer service. But she stays on the job; she feels committed to her employer, whose new company cannot afford a financial disaster precipitated by an inexperienced employee unfamiliar with the computer system. That possibility was almost a reality when six applicants either walked out before finishing the training period (they did not like the work) or left to go to a better job offer (the reason they gave). And so a conscientious church member stays on until the right person is hired and adequately trained. I have the privilege of being the pastor-servant of that servant of God whose parish is, in John Wesley's words, "the world." But all my stories (concluding with this one), plus examples and ample illustrations, only fired the laywoman's anger.

Then I realized why she was so adamant in her protest. Her reaction was to the office of pastor; to her, clergy are a hindrance to the ministry of the laity. If she could redesign the church, she would have only one office; all would be laity.

Her conversation, from which I was released by someone who came along and invited her to have a soda, exercising a ministry to me at that moment, helped me to recall a similar protest raised ten years earlier at a retreat for clergywomen. Most were unemployed or underemployed, filled with reasons to be angry and resentful. Their conclusion and solution was abolish the office of pastor, abandon the practice of ordination. Save clergywomen the despair of being unable to practice their ministry by eliminating all distinctions in ministry. In Gillian Syniatynski's words, quoted in the March 1986 issue of the United Church of Canada's *The Observer,* "the charge, today, is that many more women in ministry feel they can't accept the rules of the game. They have a different vision for the church, a way of working that wants to 'turn the ladders and hierarchies on their side.'" This person speaks for clergywomen who advocate no distinction between clergy and laity. Their hurts and protests have taught me to be aware of churches that have either neglected to correct or chosen to practice the idea that ministry is ordered through titles and ranks. This was the practice that formed the laywoman's impression and, therefore, her protest.

The same impression was personalized by a young woman who, at the age of thirteen, showed interest in becoming a pastor. Her announcement filled her parents with joy and silent pride, especially her father, who is a pastor. As high school years passed and college was almost completed, I met with the student and began to talk about seminary. "What were her choices?" Her response silenced me with disappointment. "I'm not going to seminary. I can't become a pastor; I can't be above a guy!" In college she had been introduced to the ministry as titles and ranks, and to the fundamentalist edict that women are not included in the order beyond the level of laity. To be a pastor was to rule over others! This understanding of the office of laity *under* the office of pastor and its expression in the practice of ministry had changed a pretheological student's plans. She had submitted to an order that the soda-sipping laywoman rejected. Both women became my introduction to an imperative: a different definition of Christian service, one free of titles and ranks, yet expressive of the offices inherited from the early church. What is *that* model for Christian ministry?

THE ORDER OF MINISTRY

I had to take a walk through our church's nursery department to find the answer to the above question. A toy! Colored plastic circles, diminishing in size, placed on a plastic spindle mounted to a base so each circle would stay in place—the ministry as perceived by the protesting laywoman and the submissive student. A hierarchy, with the poor laity on the bottom, providing the base, doing all the work, bearing all the weight, supporting all the orders above them; their source of resources in time, talent, treasury! And then there are the special laity, elected (perhaps ordained) to an office in the congregation, followed by the clergy in their own ascending order: pastors, professors, missionaries, bishops, archbishops (or judicatory executives), all looking to the "top"—pope, patriarch, president. The "geometry of the ministry" is made up of offices like conical sections, increasing in importance as each diminishes in size, an impression preserved in church history, perpetuated in church polity, and practiced in church "politics"! This unbiblical impression was toppled by another geometric design that sent me looking for another toy. I found it in our game closet: a box filled with plastic straws, and plugs used to join straw to straw.

They became a model for "the body," the church described in the New Testament letter to the Ephesians (4:11–12, 15b, TEV):

He [Christ] appointed some to be apostles, others to be prophets, others to be evangelists, others to be pastors and teachers. He did this to prepare all God's people for the work of Christian service, in order to build up the body of Christ . . . to Christ, who is the head.

I modeled the base of "the body" with four straws of equal length, each held together with a plastic plug (strengthened with some wire ties borrowed from plastic bags). It was a square with each corner representing an office of the ministry. In New Testament words, one corner for "prophets," another for "evangelists," another for "pastors," another for "teachers." In today's orders the names may change to "laity," "clergy," and the different expressions of each, with each being represented as a corner and each dependent on the other. Remove one corner and the square ceases to be a square, the base no longer exists. Then I joined a straw at each corner and pulled the four together to make an outline of a pyramid. It was a symbolic representation of "Christ, the head," with all the offices of the ministry looking to Christ, the only "top," and the point by which each corner has access to another corner—the biblical lesson taught through a child's game, a tool to illustrate the unranked orders of service in, through, and beyond the church; a design that "turns the ladders and hierarchies on their side." It is a lesson that prompts me to ask if the document *Baptism, Eucharist, and Ministry* could be used to teach a vertical rather than a horizontal order for ministry. The social pressures alone may be too strong, for straws are a fragile model for ministry, much more fragile than plastic cones held in place by a spindle.

Some of my ecumenical involvements have been my introduction to the pressures that threaten the description in Ephesians 4 of ministry and its unranked orders. One traumatic introduction was the firing of a capable executive of a mission agency, a firing prompted by the executive's commitment to Christian service modeled in straws, not plastic cones. But his overseas associates did not share his commitment; they saw their positions in the church as a rank they would never attain in a society in which people were locked into a class passed on from one generation to the next. They turned the ministry into a ladder; each rung was a rank and title for which to strive, through merit, threats, and payoffs. As the executive stepped down from his office, he admitted that his overseas colleagues found in the service of the church an opportunity to experience the prestige and power denied them in their country's closed social order. My years on a denominational regional staff taught me that ecclesiastical climbing is universal. In inner city or open country, small church or large church, offices in the church were and are turned into opportunities to gain recognition, to flaunt power, to be in charge. Just as some clergywomen are repulsed by this abuse of the ministry, I suspect other women may use it to attain status.

I wonder if the third section of *Baptism, Eucharist, and Ministry* could be used to legitimate an ecclesiastical hierarchy, a concern that will prove to be unfounded only if the section on baptism is not separated from the one on ministry. The first section saves ministry from becoming a hierarchy as it speaks of baptism's "images" which include the following:

The Gift of the Holy Spirit
God bestows upon all baptized persons the anointing and the presence of the Holy Spirit.   (Baptism. II. C.5)

Incorporation into the Body of Christ
Baptism is a sign and seal of our common discipleship. . . . We are one people and are called to confess and serve one Lord in each place and in all the world.   (Baptism. II. D.6)

Baptism is each Christian's response to God's gift of life in Christ, which for those of us baptized as infants is expressed in our confirmation, with the emphasis being every Christian's call to "confess and serve one Lord." Servant. This is *the* definition of ministry.

A SERVANT PEOPLE

"Servant" is the word a student's inquiry turned into a lesson that begins with Jesus and a scene from his ministry:

He rose from the table, took off his outer garment, and tied a towel around his waist. Then he poured some water into a washbasin and began to wash the disciples' feet and to dry them with the towel around his waist. . . .

After Jesus had washed their feet, he put his outer garment back on and returned to his place at the table. "Do you understand what I have just done to you?" he asked. "You call me Teacher and Lord, and it is right that you do so, because that is what I am. . . . I have set an example for you, so that you will do just what I have done for you. . . . Now that you know this truth, how happy you will be if you put it into practice!"

—John 13:4–5, 12–13, 15, 17, TEV

Verse 17 adds, "How happy you will be if you put it into practice!" Practicing all the offices of the ministry as servants makes the word servant a noun and the particular ministry an adjective, so that there are laity-servants and clergy-servants, pastor-servants and bishop-servants, yes, and pope-servant, to begin a list that is as long as there are titles and offices of ministry.

As I announced to a student that I practice my ministry as a "servant," I heard myself defining my servant role. I am a servant of the servants of God, who are the laity, in Celia Allison Hah's words in *Lay Voices in an Open Church*, "the Open Church, the Church in the World." When all expressions of ministry originate in Christ, the Servant, identified in the Servant Poems in the book of Isaiah and pictured in that table scene in the Gospel of John, the offices and titles of ministry cease being signs of status, and the tension between clergy and laity is eliminated. Each and all are servants, with service defined by the work each does. "Servant" is the word traced back to Christ, who inspires and legitimates all forms of Christian service. "Servant," is the title that spares the young woman the need to say, "I can't be above a guy!" "Servant" is the word that should answer the angry laywoman's protest and the clergywomen's commitment to turning ecclesiastical hierarchies on their sides, from plastic cones to straws!

It all happens through Christ's words, "I have set an example for you." Christ is a Christian's model for ministry. When a student prompted me to express that definition, I felt the thrill of learning (like Albert Schweitzer's unforeseen, unsought phrase) "reverence for life." I had been introduced to the joy of a word for laity and clergy in the community called "Christian." Christ, modeling the word servant, imparts a reverence to every Christian's ministry.

The happiness of that practice of ministry is also the joy of finding a title that is inclusive. The word servant not only lacks status, but is also free of bias or gender preference. Servants have no occasions to quibble over pronouns! I find that to be an exciting alternative to all the traditional terms for clergy that, just by being named, conjure exclusively male images of the ordained ministry. I am also excited about the word's elimination of any order of clergy over laity. "Servant" is the word that holds the potential of introducing ordained and unordained to each other. I feel the thrill of pursuing that introduction with laity as well as with my clergy sisters and brothers. The thrill is the exploration of our common ministry and all we'll learn as we let the word servant teach us who we are.

ONE MORE LESSON

Credit for one more lesson goes to Deborah Streeter and her words in *Journal of Women and Religion* (Vol. 4, No. 1, Winter 1984). She ended her editorial with these words: "Each Sunday as I prepare for worship, I put on my own 'fabric of faith.' Over my robe I place a simple blue vest-

97

ment, panels of cloth front and back connected over the shoulders. People ask me if 'my blue thing' has a name, and I say yes, it is my apron." She describes the caring work of women as their "religious acts" for which an apron has been their traditional "vestment." Deborah Streeter identified her "blue thing" as her "apron of religious leadership and service."

The Sunday after that editorial was read I opened the closet door in the Pastor's Study, took out my robe with its white tabs, put it on, fastened the buttons, and then reached for the stole with the color that was appropriate for that Sunday in the church year. As I held the strip of cloth in my hand I thought, "A stole, the sign of ordination to the Christian ministry, worn by some as a mark of distinction, an announcement of rank, a narrow scarf only the clergy are privileged to wear." Then I remembered a stole's origin: a scarf worn when traveling in warm climates where it was used to drive away insects and wipe the face clean of sweat and dirt, a piece of cloth that became a standard part of clergy apparel from the seventh century on, and therefore a sign to distinguish clergy from laity. A scarf was used as a towel. The word towel turned my thoughts to that Gospel scene, Christ with a basin, and a towel fastened to his waist like an apron, doing a servant's work. A stole is not a mark of a privileged order, the clergy; it is a servant's apparel, worn by those who are in the service of the Servant-Christ. A stole is a clergyperson's towel!

My stole is a towel! I had just assimilated one more lesson taught by another clergywoman ministering to me through words about her "fabric of faith." My stole is a towel! I find that thought to be just as exciting as the word servant. And just as challenging! For how many years have clergymen (and the gender is intentional) put on the stole, the sign of their office, never identifying it as a towel, a sign of service? Now clergywomen, for whom a towel worn as an apron has been their traditional garment for "women's work," can model a stole's full meaning: a pastor's towel!

"Stole" is a strip of cloth that makes the pastoral office inclusive, for it is the towel of service designed to be worn by clergymen and clergywomen. "Servant" is the word that makes all offices and expressions of ministry an unranked service, for it is the title intended for every baptized Christian. These are lessons waiting to be taught by women and men whose classroom is a congregation and whose life is the curriculum. My prayer for my ministry is that I may be a servant (pastor) of the servants of God (laity), equipping them for their ministry in the world.

CONCLUSION

Visibility, identity, realities, acceptability, charity, ministry are names of invisible threads woven into a pastor's stole, a towel I am still learning how to wear. I have tried to identify my own classrooms, curriculum, and instructors so that others may look for each in their own time and place, and do more—become a teacher of someone else. Until now I have neglected the service of describing those invisible threads, an omission I confess and correct as almost thirty years of silence end with personal notes and observations turned into chapters.

"Lessons learned in the parish ministry" are thoughts that race through my mind whenever I raise my stole over my head and lower it on my shoulders, a sign of a ministry others have taught me to perform as a servant. A piece of cloth that marks me as one who is in the service of the Servant-Christ.

This book is dedicated to sisters and brothers whose mark of service is a stole; to women and men who are waiting to put on a pastor's towel; and to mentors, family, colleagues, congregations whose lessons teach me how to wear what was once a scarf to chase away insects, a towel to wipe off sweat, as a sign of the office of the pastoral ministry. A stole is a towel!

APPENDIX

•

ASSIGNMENTS & QUIZZES

Classrooms and lessons mean assignments and quizzes. These are designed to be adaptable to each reader's experience and practice of ministry: denominational or judicatory personnel, clergypersons, laity, seminarians. These assignments and quizzes are also flexible; they may be used by groups or individuals, in a class or study group, as a formal project or as a personal exercise in learning. The intention is to encourage another's ministry and to discover, appreciate, practice one's own—as a servant of the Servant-Christ.

Read: *Women of the Cloth* by Jackson W. Carroll, Barbara Hargrove, and Adair T. Lummis (San Francisco: Harper & Row, 1981). Relate its chapters, interviews, research to the "lessons."

Send to your denomination's national office for research on women seminarians and clergy; ask for everything that is available and then complete this quiz.

What is available on the subject of
1. seminary courses and counsel for women?
2. denominational and judicatory guidelines for placing women seminarians in parishes and women clergy as pastors?
3. guidelines for pastoral search committees? Do they include equal consideration (of women as well as men), a process for evaluating dossiers and screening candidates,

a committee's sharing of prejudices and myths and facts to correct them, and a standard format for the interview?

―――――――

Study your denomination's material for clergy and then complete this quiz.

What is provided for
  1. clergy self-evaluation?
  2. a congregation's self-evaluation?
  3. guidelines for the pastoral ministry?
  4. resources for the effective leadership of clergy and laity?
  5. the interrelatedness of ministries, lay and ordained?
  6. data on sexual harassment—statistics, counsel, support groups for victims?

What is your denomination's definition of the offices of the ministry (based on material available)?
  1. Does the material encourage women as well as men to be pastors?
  2. Using the material, write a job description for a pastor and a definition of ministry, laity, and clergy.

―――――――

"Adopt a seminarian" in your church, woman or man, but alternating each time; or share in that adoption with another church.

―――――――

Keep a file of books, magazine articles, newspaper clippings on
  1. positive examples of women serving in the ordained ministry;
  2. negative experiences;
  3. actions to affirm women's ministries in your church, other churches, and denominations;
  4. reactions to women's ministries.

Using this collected material, ascertain the trend geographically, denominationally, theologically, toward women in ministry.

———

Take a tour around the neighborhood or town or city; visit churches with different histories, traditions, and "personalities in the pulpit." Write a job description of a clergyperson, based on observations from your visits.

If, in the churches you observed, there are clergywomen as well as clergymen, note the following:
1. Differences in conduct of ministry
2. Differences in leadership style
From your observations, could you say that women went about the work of pastor in the same way, or in a different way, from men? If different, what were the differences?

———

Invite clergy, women and men, to tell their "story" of their reasons for entering the ministry, their joys and problems, the prejudices they experienced.

———

Invite laypeople to identify their ministries in church, home, work, world.

On Labor, Stewardship, or Church Vocations Sunday, celebrate ministry—*everyone's* ministry. Have the offering be a procession of symbols of the congregation's vocations brought forward with the regular offering.

———

Use the Bible references of the "lessons" and the biblical references in material secured from your denomination as the resource for Bible study on
1. scripture's examples of women as well as men engaged in ministry;
2. the varieties and form of ministries.

Turn research into chancel drama and choral readings for services of worship.

DATE DUE

HIGHSMITH   #LO-45220